AMAZING WORLD FACTS

Terry O'Brien is an esteemed academician and an ardent quiz aficionado. He is keenly interested in kindling the quizzing instinct in people and an aptitude to develop the 3Rs of learning: Read, Record, and Recall. He is a trainers' instructor and a motivational speaker. He has penned a number of books. He is very well known for his flair for speaking and his articulating abilities in writing.

Bestsellers by the Author

CATEGORY I

Language skills for all age groups from class 3 onwards: The Little Red Book series.

CATEGORY II

For beginners: *A Child's First Dictionary* (The Little Red Book series).

CATEGORY III

To develop a love for reading among schoolchildren and also for adults, a collection of the best stories by renowned writers: The Masterpieces of World Fiction series.

CATEGORY IV

For developing quiz instinct and general awareness: The Fun Fact series—*Fun with Numbers, Fun with Riddles,* etc.; *A2Z Quiz Book; The Book of Firsts and Lasts.*

CATEGORY V

Motivational books: *The Book of Virtues* and *The Book of Motivation.*

CATEGORY VI

For overall preparation and general awareness: *The Students' Companion.*

CATEGORY VII

Teachers' reference book: *A2Z Book of Word Origins.*

AMAZING WORLD FACTS

TERRY O'BRIEN

Published by
Rupa Publications India Pvt. Ltd 2016
7/16, Ansari Road, Daryaganj
New Delhi 110 002

Sales Centres:
Allahabad Bengaluru Chennai
Hyderabad Jaipur Kathmandu
Kolkata Mumbai

Copyright © Terry O'Brien 2016

The views and opinions expressed in this book are the author's own and the facts are as reported by him which have been verified to the extent possible, and the publishers are not in any way liable for the same.

All rights reserved.
No part of this publication may be reproduced, stored in a retrieval system, or transmitted, in any form or by any means, electronic, mechanical, photocopying, recording or otherwise, without the prior permission of the publishers.

ISBN : 978-81-291-3990-0

Eighth impression 2022

10 9 8

The author asserts the moral right to be
identified as the author of this work.

Typeset by Innovative Processors, New Delhi

Printed in India

This book is sold subject to the condition that it shall not, by way of trade or otherwise, be lent, resold, hired out, or otherwise circulated, without the publisher's prior consent, in any form of binding or cover other than that in which it is published.

Introduction

Kids always show great interest in knowing some extraordinary and unknown facts that they have never heard about before. It may be about animals, plants or any places in the world or in nature. Kids are very curious to know about such amazing facts. By knowing details of such facts they can increase their knowledge wealth.

Knowledge is power. Learning new things every day help us grow in many ways. Irrespective of the new aspects we learn, there is massive amount that remains to be learnt. Known things and unknown facts are the concept of this book. Here come many interesting and surprising facts from different segments. We live in Earth, but Earth is the only planet in the solar system that is not named after a god. Ever thought about this fact? Quite surprising! From language, animals, climate, geography, science, plants, daily habits, social elements, education, this book covers a wide range of categories to provide the unknown or lesser-known facts! Here comes a little boost to your knowledge! These tiny pieces of Amazing World Facts are a simple step to educate your children, a bit extra about what they already are aware. The book would like to educate the readers to learn something new every day! Of course, excessive knowledge cost you nothing.

Happy reading!
Terry O'Brien

Contents

	Introduction	v
1.	Space Facts	1
2.	Water World	28
3.	The Plant World	49
4.	Bird Kingdom	56
5.	Insect World	64
6.	Mountain World	69
7.	Cities of the World	73
8.	Languages of the World	97
9.	Religions	104
10.	Food	112
11.	Sports	118
12.	World Literature	129

1 Space Facts

The Amazing Star World

- It would take 70,000 years to travel from earth to the nearest star outside our solar system.
- Almost every star in the Milky Way has at least one planet orbiting it.
- Stars have a life cycle of birth, growth and death.
- Different parts of the sun rotate at different speeds.
- Billions of years after some stars die, they turn into Diamonds!
- Stars don't really twinkle; they just look that way from earth.
- The fastest stars in the milky way, known as hypervelocity stars, travel 530 miles every second.
- Sirius, the brightest star in our night sky, is often mistaken for a UFO.
- Stars you see at night look small but are actually bigger than the sun.
- The largest known star could be 1,800 times larger than our sun.
- You can see 2,500 stars at one time.
- Only four million galaxies are visible to the naked eye.
- But generally you can only see two; and one of those is the Milky Way—this is where we are.
- There are more than 100 billion galaxies in the universe, each containing between 10 and 100 billion stars.
- In the Northern Hemisphere, you can see the Milky Way and Andromeda.

- In the Southern Hemisphere you can see the Large and Small Magellanic Clouds.
- 10,000 stars are visible to the naked eye.
- There are about 50 billion stars in the Milky Way.
- The moon is roughly the same size as Earth.
- Earth's moon is slowly drifting away from our planet.
- The Sun will continue to shine for another 5 billion years.
- A day on the moon is more than 600 hours long.
- A solar eclipse—when the moon is exactly between the Earth and sun—lasts for 7 minutes.
- 609 hours, 7 minutes is a day on the sun in Earth time.
- The moon orbits the Earth.
- Earth orbits the sun.
- The constellation Gemini is supposed to look like twins.
- Stars are being born in the Orion Nebula. It looks like a strangely shaped cloud.
- The stars only seem to line up when viewed from Earth. Actually, the stars of almost all constellations are in very different locations in space.
- Stars move through space, but because they are so far away, they seem fixed in place. In 50,000 years, some constellations will look different.
- Zodiac signs are constellations that fall on a band that seems to move around Earth as it rotates on its axis. Over the centuries, the timing has changed so that the traditional calendar of the Zodiac is not accurate any more.
- If you walk toward Polaris, the Pole Star, you will be going north direction.
- The oldest surviving paper map of the stars comes from China.
- The nickname of Sirius, the brightest star in the sky is the Dog Star.

> **INSIDE OUT**
>
> Sirius is also well known as the Dog Star, because it is the chief star in the constellation Canis Major, the Big Dog. Sirius is behind the sun as seen from Earth in Northern Hemisphere summer. In late summer, it appears in the east before sunrise—near the sun in our sky.

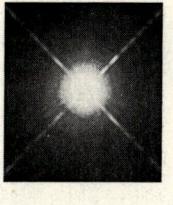

Galaxy Quest

- The Apollo astronauts who landed on the moon all claimed that moon dust smelled like gunpowder.
- In China astronauts are called 'cosmonauts'.
- In Space, burps come out wet.
- In space, liquids form tiny Spheres, or balls.
- If a battle took place in Space, it would be very loud.
- Your weight would be one-sixth of what is it on the earth on the moon.
- Venus is the hottest planet in the solar system.
- Venus is the only planet in our solar system that spins backward.
- Millions of pieces of space junk spin around the Earth at a speed of 15,000 miles an hour.
- One piece of space debris falls back to Earth every day.
- Scientists are currently working on a gravity tractor that will be used to keep near-Earth objects from crashing to our surface.
- 'Lucy' is the nickname of the largest diamond in our galaxy as a star.
- A day on Mercury is equal to about two Earth months.
- It snows on Mars.

Galaxy Far, Far Away

The Hubble Space Telescope has spotted the most distant galaxy yet. It is so far away that the light from this cluster of stars has taken 13.4 billion years to reach us.

- The faint cluster of stars has been named Gn-z11 and is located in the direction of the Ursa Major constellation.
- Owing to its distance from the Earth, Hubble sees the galaxy as it was 400 million years after the Big Bang.
- 25 times is by how much GNz11 is smaller than the Milky Way.
- Astronauts say finding this galaxy is an extraordinary accomplishment for the 25 year old Hubble, the record can only be broken by its successor James Webb Telescope to launch in 2018.

> **INSIDE OUT**
> A team of international scientists has discovered 883 galaxies hidden from view until now by the Milky Way, some 250 million light years away from the earth.

Saturn's Secrets

- Saturn is the least dense planet in the solar system.
- More than 163 earths would fit into Saturn.
- Summer on Saturn lasts about seven earth years.
- Saturn is more than 74 million miles (1.3 billion km) from earth.
- It's impossible to live on Saturn, because its surface is made mostly of gas.
- Each ring travels around Saturn at a different speed.

- The rings of Saturn are the most extensive planetary ring system of any planet in the Solar System.
- They consist of countless small particles, ranging in size from micrometres to metres that orbit about Saturn.
- Saturn's rings are made mostly of ice.
- Saturn's rings stretch into space.
- The winds on Saturn blow at about 1,118 miles an hour—five times faster than the strongest winds on Earth!
- Saturn has 62 moons.
- If it were possible to go from earth to Saturn, the journey would take more than 30,000 years!
- The average temperature on Saturn is -288°F.
- It took one spacecraft nearly seven years to get to Saturn.
- Saturn is naturally beige; coloured camera filters are used to make its colours brighter and details more visible.
- A day on Saturn is 10 hours, 14 minutes long.
- Saturn would float in water.

> **INSIDE OUT**
>
> Saturn is sometimes called 'The Jewel of the Solar System'. It is a planet that is nothing like our own. Humans have been gazing up at Saturn for a long time. They have been wondering about it for thousands of years.

All Planet Facts

There are 8 planets in our solar system: Mercury, Venus, Earth, Mars, Jupiter, Saturn, Uranus and Neptune. With the exception of Neptune and Uranus the other 6 planets can be seen unaided and all 8 are visible with a small telescope or binoculars.

Earth

- Earth is the third planet from the Sun and is the largest of the terrestrial planets.

- The Earth is the only planet in our solar system not to be named after a Greek or Roman deity. The other seven planets in our solar system are all named after Roman gods or goddesses. Although only Mercury, Venus, Mars, Jupiter and Saturn were named during ancient times, because they were visible to the naked eye, the Roman method of naming planets was retained after the discovery of Uranus and Neptune.
- The Earth was formed approximately 4.54 billion years ago and is the only known planet to support life.
- The Equatorial Diameter of the earth is 12,756 km; its Polar Diameter is 12,714 km. The earth has one Moon.
- The Earth's rotation is gradually slowing: This deceleration is happening almost imperceptibly, at approximately 17 milliseconds per hundred years, although the rate at which it occurs is not perfectly uniform. This has the effect of lengthening our days, but it happens so slowly that it could be as much as 140 million years before the length of a day will have increased to 25 hours.
- Earth has a powerful magnetic field: This phenomenon is caused by the nickel-iron core of the planet, coupled with its rapid rotation. This field protects the Earth from the effects of solar wind.
- There is only one natural satellite of the planet Earth: As a percentage of the size of the body it orbits, the Moon is the largest satellite of any planet in our solar system. In real terms, however, it is only the fifth largest natural satellite.
- The Earth is the densest planet in the Solar System: This varies according to the part of the planet; for example, the metallic core is denser than the crust. The average density of the Earth is approximately 5.52 grams per cubic centimetre.
- 70 per cent of the Earth's surface is covered in water: When astronauts first went into the space, they looked back at the Earth with human eyes for the first time, and called our home the Blue Planet. And it's no surprise. 70 per cent of our planet is covered with oceans. The remaining 30 per cent is the solid

ground, rising above sea level.
- Earth is mostly iron, oxygen and silicon: If you could separate the Earth out into piles of material, you'd get 32.1 per cent iron, 30.1 per cent oxygen, 15.1 per cent silicon, and 13.9 per cent magnesium. Of course, most of this iron is actually down at the core of the Earth. If you could actually get down and sample the core, it would be 88 per cent iron. 47 per cent of the Earth's crust consists of oxygen.
- Earth doesn't take 24 hours to rotate on its axis: It's actually 23 hours, 56 minutes and 4 seconds. This is the amount of time it takes for the Earth to completely rotate around its axis; astronomers call this a sidereal day.
- A year on Earth isn't 365 days: It's actually 365.2564 days. This extra .2564 days that creates the need for leap years. That's why we tack on an extra day in February every year.
- Earth has 1 moon and 2 co-orbital satellites.
- Earth has 1 moon (The Moon). There are 2 additional asteroids locked into a co-orbital orbits with Earth—3753 Cruithne and 2002 AA29. 3753 Cruithne is 5 km across, and sometimes called Earth's second moon. It doesn't actually orbit the Earth, but has a synchronized orbit with our home planet. It has an orbit that makes it look like it's following the Earth in orbit, but it's actually following its own, distinct path around the Sun.
- 2002 AA29 is only 60 meters across, and makes a horseshoe orbit around the Earth that brings it close to the planet every 95 years. In about 600 years, it will appear to circle Earth in a quasi-satellite orbit. Scientists have suggested that it might make a good target for a space exploration mission.
- The Earth is not actually round in shape; in fact it is geoid. This simply means that the rounded shape has a slight bulge towards the equator. So what causes this geoid shape? This happens solely because the rotation of the Earth which causes the bulge around the equator.
- The Earth tilts at roughly 66 degrees. Only 3 per cent water of the earth is fresh, rest 97 per cent salted. Of that 3 per cent,

over 2 per cent is frozen in ice sheets and glaciers. Means less than 1 per cent fresh water is found in lakes, rivers and underground.

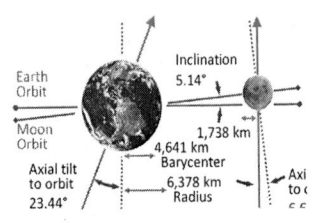

- Asia Continent is covered 30 per cent of the total earth land area, but represent 60 per cent of the world's population.
- Each winter there are about 1 septillion (1, 000, 000, 000, 000, 000, 000, 000, 000 or a trillion trillion) snow crystals that drop from the sky.

Mars

Mars is the fourth planet from the Sun. Named after the Roman god of war, and often described as the 'Red Planet' due to its reddish appearance, Mars is a terrestrial planet with a thin atmosphere composed primarily of carbon dioxide.

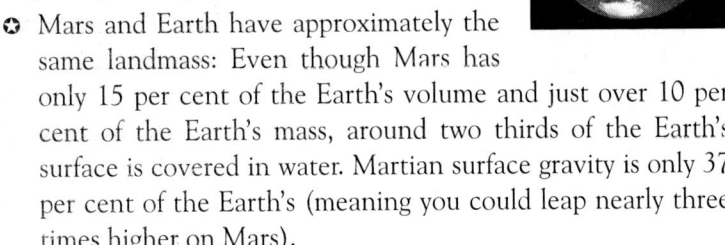

- Mars and Earth have approximately the same landmass: Even though Mars has only 15 per cent of the Earth's volume and just over 10 per cent of the Earth's mass, around two thirds of the Earth's surface is covered in water. Martian surface gravity is only 37 per cent of the Earth's (meaning you could leap nearly three times higher on Mars).
- Mars is home to the tallest mountain in the solar system: Olympus Mons, a shield volcano, is 21 km high and 600 km in diameter. Despite having formed over billions of years, evidence from volcanic lava flows is so recent many scientists believe it could still be active.
- Only 18 missions to Mars have been successful.
- As of September 2014 there have been 40 missions to Mars, including orbiters, landers and rovers but not counting flybys. The most recent arrivals include the Mars Curiosity mission in 2012, the Maven mission, which arrived on September 22,

2014, followed by the Indian Space Research Organization's MOM Mangalyaan orbiter, which arrived on September 24, 2014. The next missions to arrive will be the European Space Agency's ExoMars mission, comprising an orbiter, lander, and a rover, followed by NASA's InSight robotic lander mission, slated for launch in March 2016 and a planned arrival in September, 2016.

- Mars has the largest dust storms in the solar system: They can last for months and cover the entire planet. The seasons are extreme because its elliptical (oval-shaped) orbital path around the Sun is more elongated than most other planets in the solar system.
- On Mars the Sun appears about half the size as it does on Earth: At the closest point to the Sun, the Martian southern hemisphere leans towards the Sun, causing a short, intensely hot summer, while the northern hemisphere endures a brief, cold winter: at its farthest point from the Sun, the Martian northern hemisphere leans towards the Sun, causing a long, mild summer, while the southern hemisphere endures a lengthy, cold winter.

Jupiter

The planet Jupiter is the fifth planet out from the Sun, and is two and a half times more massive than all the other planets in the solar system combined. It is made primarily of gases and is therefore known as a 'gas giant'.

- Jupiter is the fourth brightest object in the solar system: Only the Sun, Moon and Venus are brighter. It is one of five planets visible to the naked eye from Earth.
- The ancient Babylonians were the first to record their sightings of Jupiter: This was around the 7th or 8th century BC. Jupiter is named after the king of the Roman gods. To the Greeks, it represented Zeus, the god of thunder. The

Mesopotamians saw Jupiter as the god Marduk and patron of the city of Babylon. Germanic tribes saw this planet as Donar, or Thor.

- Jupiter has the shortest day of all the planets: It turns on its axis once every 9 hours and 55 minutes. The rapid rotation flattens the planet slightly, giving it an oblate shape.
- Jupiter orbits the Sun once every 11.8 Earth years: From our point of view on Earth, it appears to move slowly in the sky, taking months to move from one constellation to another.

Saturn

Saturn is the sixth planet from the Sun and the most distant that can be seen with the naked eye. It is best known for its fabulous ring system that was discovered in 1610 by the astronomer Galileo Galilei.

- Saturn can be seen with the naked eye: It is the fifth brightest object in the solar system and is also easily studied through binoculars or a small telescope.
- Saturn was known to the ancients, including the Babylonians and Far Eastern observers: It is named for the Roman god Saturnus, and was known to the Greeks as Cronus.
- Saturn is the flattest planet: Its polar diameter is 90 per cent of its equatorial diameter, this is due to its low density and fast rotation. Saturn turns on its axis once every 10 hours and 34 minutes giving it the second-shortest day of any of the solar system's planets.
- Saturn orbits the Sun once every 29.4 Earth years: Its slow movement against the backdrop of stars earned it the nickname of 'Lubadsagush' from the ancient Assyrians. The name means 'oldest of the old'.
- Saturn has oval-shaped storms similar to Jupiter's: The region around its north pole has a hexagonal-shaped pattern of clouds. Scientists think this may be a wave pattern in the upper clouds. The planet also has a vortex over its south pole

that resembles a hurricane-like storm.
- Saturn is made mostly of hydrogen: It exists in layers that get denser farther into the planet. Eventually, deep inside, the hydrogen becomes metallic. At the core lies a hot interior.
- Saturn has the most extensive rings in the solar system: The Saturnian rings are made mostly of chunks of ice and small amounts of carbonaceous dust. The rings stretch out more than 120,700 km from the planet, but are are amazingly thin; only about 20 meters thick.
- Saturn has 62 moons and smaller moonlets: All are frozen worlds. The largest moons are Titan and Rhea. Enceladus appears to have an ocean below its frozen surface.
- Titan is a moon with complex and dense nitrogen-rich atmosphere: It is composed mostly of water ice and rock. Its frozen surface has lakes of liquid methane and landscapes covered with frozen nitrogen. Planetary scientists consider Titan to be a possible harbour for life, but not Earth-like life.
- Four spacecraft have visited Saturn: Pioneer 11, Voyager 1 and 2, and the Cassini-Huygens mission have all studied the planet. Cassini continues to orbit Saturn, sending back a wealth of data about the planet, its moons, and rings.

Uranus

Uranus is the seventh planet from the Sun. It's not visible to the naked eye, and became the first planet discovered with the use of a telescope. Uranus is tipped over on its side with an axial tilt of 98 degrees. It is often described as 'rolling around the Sun on its side'.

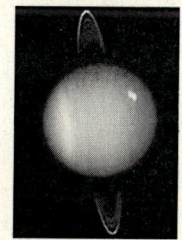

- Uranus was officially discovered by Sir William Herschel in 1781: It is too dim to have been seen by the ancients. At first Herschel thought it was a comet, but several years later it was confirmed as a planet. Herscal tried to have his discovery named 'Georgian Sidus' after King George III. The name Uranus was suggested by astronomer Johann Bode. The name comes from the ancient Greek deity Ouranos.

- Uranus turns on its axis once every 17 hours, 14 minutes: The planet rotates in a retrograde direction, opposite to the way Earth and most other planets turn.
- Uranus makes one trip around the Sun every 84 Earth years: During some parts of its orbit one or the other of its poles point directly at the Sun and get about 42 years of direct sunlight. The rest of the time they are in darkness.
- Uranus is often referred to as an 'ice giant' planet: Like the other gas giants, it has a hydrogen upper layer, which has helium mixed in. Below that is an icy mantle, which surrounds a rock and ice core. The upper atmosphere is made of water, ammonia and the methane ice crystals that give the planet its pale blue color.
- Uranus hits the coldest temperatures of any planet: With minimum atmospheric temperature of -224°C Uranus is nearly coldest planet in the solar system. While Neptune doesn't get as cold as Uranus it is on average colder. The upper atmosphere of Uranus is covered by a methane haze which hides the storms that take place in the cloud decks.
- Uranus has two sets of rings of very thin set of dark colored rings: The ring particles are small, ranging from a dust-sized particles to small boulders. There are eleven inner rings and two outer rings. They probably formed when one or more of Uranus's moons were broken up in an impact. The first rings were discovered in 1977 with the two outer rings being discovered in Hubble Space Telescope images between 2003 and 2005.
- Uranus' moons are named after characters created by William Shakespeare and Alaxander Pope: These include Oberon, Titania and Miranda. All are frozen worlds with dark surfaces. Some are ice and rock mixtures. The most interesting Uranian moon is Miranda; it has ice canyons, terraces, and other strange-looking surface areas.
- Only one spacecraft has flown by Uranus: In 1986, the Voyager

2 spacecraft swept past the planet at a distance of 81,500 km. It returned the first close-up images of the planet, its moons, and rings.

Venus

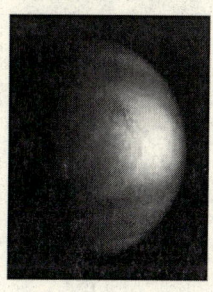

Venus is the second planet from the Sun and is the second brightest object in the night sky after the Moon. Named after the Roman goddess of love and beauty, Venus is the second largest terrestrial planet and is sometimes referred to as the Earth's sister planet due the their similar size and mass. The surface of the planet is obscured by an opaque layer of clouds made up of sulfuric acid.

- A day on Venus lasts longer than a year: It takes 243 Earth days to rotate once on its axis. The planet's orbit around the Sun takes 225 Earth days, compared to the Earth's 365.
- Venus is often called the Earth's sister planet: The Earth and Venus are very similar in size with only a 638 km difference in diameter, Venus having 81.5 per cent of the Earth's mass. Both also have a central core, a molten mantle and a crust.
- Venus rotates in the opposite direction to most other planets: This means that Venus is rotating in the opposite direction to the Sun, this is also know as a retrograde rotation. A possible reason might be a collision in the past with an asteroid or other object that caused the planet to alter its rotational path. It also differs from most other planets in our solar system by having no natural satellites.
- Venus is the second brightest object in the night sky: Only the Moon is brighter. With a magnitude of between -3.8 to -4.6 Venus is so bright it can be seen during daytime on a clear day.
- Atmospheric pressure on Venus is 92 times greater than the Earth's: While its size and mass are similar to Earth, the small asteroids are crushed when entering its atmosphere, meaning no small craters lie on the surface of the planet. The pressure

felt by a human on the surface would be equivalent to that experienced deep beneath the sea on Earth.
- Venus is also known as the Morning Star and the Evening Star: Early civilisations thought Venus was two different bodies, called Phosphorus and Hesperus by the Greeks, and Lucifer and Vesper by the Romans. This is because when its orbit around the Sun overtakes Earth's orbit, it changes from being visible after sunset to being visible before sunrise. Mayan astronomers made detailed observations of Venus as early as 650 AD.
- Venus is the hottest planet in our solar system: The average surface temperature is 462°C, and because Venus does not tilt on its axis, there is no seasonal variation. The dense atmosphere of around 96.5 per cent carbon dioxide traps heat and causes a greenhouse effect.

Mercury

Mercury is the closest planet to the Sun and due to its proximity it is not easily seen except during twilight. For every two orbits of the Sun, Mercury completes three rotations about its axis and up until 1965 it was thought that the same side of Mercury constantly faced the Sun. Thirteen times a century Mercury can be observed from the Earth passing across the face of the Sun in an event called a transit, the next will occur on the 9th May 2016.

- A year on Mercury is just 88 days long: One solar day (the time from noon to noon on the planet's surface) on Mercury lasts the equivalent of 176 Earth days while the sidereal day (the time for 1 rotation in relation to a fixed point) lasts 59 Earth days. Mercury is nearly tidally locked to the Sun and over time this has slowed the rotation of the planet to almost match its orbit around the Sun. Mercury also has the highest orbital eccentricity of all the planets with its distance from the Sun ranging from 46 to 70 million km.

- Mercury is the smallest planet in the Solar System: One of five planets visible with the naked eye a, Mercury is just 4,879 Kilometres across its equator, compared with 12,742 Kilometres for the Earth.
- Mercury is the second densest planet: Even though the planet is small, Mercury is very dense. Each cubic centimetre has a density of 5.4 grams, with only the Earth having a higher density. This is largely due to Mercury being composed mainly of heavy metals and rock.
- Mercury has wrinkles: As the iron core of the planet cooled and contracted, the surface of the planet became wrinkled. Scientist have named these wrinkles, Lobate Scarps. These Scarps can be up to a mile high and hundreds of miles long.
- Mercury has a molten core: In recent years scientists from NASA have come to believe the solid iron core of Mercury could in fact be molten. Normally the core of smaller planets cools rapidly, but after extensive research, the results were not in line with those expected from a solid core. Scientists now believe the core to contain a lighter element such as sulphur, which would lower the melting temperature of the core material. It is estimated Mercury's core makes up 42 per cent of its volume, while the Earth's core makes up 17 per cent.
- Mercury is only the second hottest planet: Despite being further from the Sun, Venus experiences higher temperatures. The surface of Mercury which faces the Sun sees temperatures of up to 427°C, whilst on the alternate side this can be as low as -173°C. This is due to the planet having no atmosphere to help regulate the temperature.

Neptune

Neptune is the eighth planet from the Sun making it the most distant in the solar system. This gas giant planet may have formed much closer to the Sun in early solar system history before migrating to its present position.

- Neptune was not known to the ancients: It is not visible to the naked eye and was first observed in 1846. Its position was determined using mathematical predictions. It was named after the Roman god of the sea.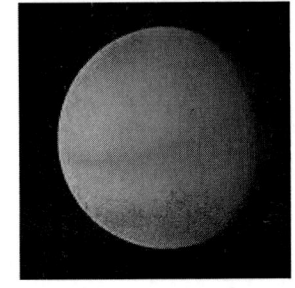
- Neptune spins on its axis very rapidly: Its equatorial clouds take 18 hours to make one rotation. This is because Neptune is not solid body.
- Neptune is the smallest of the ice giants: Despite being smaller than Uranus, Neptune has a greater mass. Below its heavy atmosphere, Uranus is made of layers of hydrogen, helium, and methane gases. They enclose a layer of water, ammonia and methane ice. The inner core of the planet is made of rock.
- The atmosphere of Neptune is made of hydrogen and helium, with some methane: The methane absorbs red light, which makes the planet appear a lovely blue. High, thin clouds drift in the upper atmosphere.
- Neptune has a very active climate: Large storms whirl through its upper atmosphere, and high-speed winds track around the planet at up 600 metres per second. One of the largest storms ever seen was recorded in 1989. It was called the Great Dark Spot. It lasted about five years.
- Neptune has a very thin collection of rings: They are likely made up of ice particles mixed with dust grains and possibly coated with a carbon-based substance.
- Neptune has 14 moons: The most interesting moon is Triton, a frozen world that is spewing nitrogen ice and dust particles out from below its surface. It was likely captured by the gravitational pull of Neptune. It is probably the coldest world in the solar system.
- Only one spacecraft has flown by Neptune: In 1989, the Voyager 2 spacecraft swept past the planet. It returned the first close-up images of the Neptune system. The NASA/ESA

Hubble Space Telescope has also studied this planet, as have a number of ground-based telescopes.

Sun Facts

Our Solar System

The Sun or Sol, is the star at the centre of our solar system and is responsible for the Earth's climate and weather. The Sun is an almost perfect sphere with a difference of just 10 km in diametre between the poles and the equator. The average radius of the Sun is 695,508 km (109.2 x that of the Earth) of which 20–25 per cent is the core.

- One million Earths could fit inside the Sun: If a hollow Sun was filled up with spherical Earths then around 960,000 would fit inside. On the other hand if these Earths were squished inside with no wasted space then around 1,300,000 would fit inside. The Sun's surface area is 11,990 times that of the Earth's.
- Eventually, the Sun will consume the Earth: When all the Hydrogen has been burned, the Sun will continue for about 130 million more years, burning Helium, during which time it will expand to the point that it will engulf Mercury and Venus and the Earth. At this stage it will have become a red giant.
- The Sun will one day be about the size of Earth: After its red giant phase, the Sun will collapse, retaining its enormous mass, but containing the approximate volume of our planet. When this happens, it will be called a white dwarf.
- The Sun contains 99.86 per cent of the mass in the Solar System: The mass of the Sun is approximately 330,000 times greater than that of Earth. It is almost three quarters Hydrogen, whilst most of the remaining mass is Helium.
- The Sun is an almost perfect sphere: There is only a 10 kilometre difference in its polar diametre compared to its equatorial diametre. Considering the vast expanse of the Sun,

this means it is the closest thing to a perfect sphere that has been observed in nature.

- Light from the Sun takes eight minutes to reach Earth: With a mean average distance of 150 million kilometres from Earth and with light travelling at 300,000 kilometres per second, dividing one by the other gives us an approximate time of 500 seconds, or eight minutes and 20 seconds. Although this energy reaches Earth in a few minutes, it will already have taken millions of years to travel from the Sun's core to its surface.
- The Sun travels at 220 kilometres per second: The Sun is 24,000–26,000 light years from the galactic centre and it takes the Sun 225–250 million years to complete an orbit of the centre of the Milky Way.
- The distance from the Sun to Earth changes throughout the year: Because the Earth travels on an elliptical orbit around the Sun, the distance between the two bodies varies from 147 to 152 million kilometres. The distance between the Earth and the Sun is called an Astronomical Unit (AU).
- The Sun is middle-aged: At around 4.5 billion years old, the Sun has already burned off about half of its store of Hydrogen. It has enough left to continue to burn Hydrogen for approximately another 5 billion years. The Sun is currently a type of star known as a Yellow Dwarf.
- The Sun has a very strong magnetic field: Solar flares occur when magnetic energy is released by the Sun during magnetic storms, which we see as sunspots. In sunspots, the magnetic lines are twisted and they spin, much like a tornado would on Earth.
- The temperature inside the Sun can reach 15 million degrees Celsius: At the Sun's core, energy is generated by nuclear fusion, as Hydrogen converts to Helium. Because hot objects generally expand, the Sun would explode like a giant bomb if it weren't for its enormous gravitational force.
- The Sun generates solar wind: This is a stream of charged particles, which travels through the Solar System at

approximately 450 kilometres per second. Solar wind occurs where the magnetic field of the Sun extends into space instead of following its surface.

THE MOON

The Moon (or Luna) is the Earth's only natural satellite and was formed 4.6 billion years ago around some 30–50 million years after the formation of the solar system. The Moon is in synchronous rotation with Earth meaning the same side is always facing the Earth. The first unmanned mission to the Moon was in 1959 by the Soviet Lunar Programme with the first manned landing being Apollo 11 in 1969.

- The dark side of the moon is a myth: In reality both sides of the Moon see the same amount of sunlight however only one face of the Moon is ever seen from Earth. This is because the Moon rotates around on its own axis in exactly the same time it takes to orbit the Earth, meaning the same side is always facing the Earth. The side facing away from Earth has only been seen by the human eye from spacecraft.
- The rise and fall of the tides on Earth is caused by the Moon: There are two bulges in the Earth due to the gravitational pull that the Moon exerts; one on the side facing the Moon, and the other on the opposite side that faces away from the Moon, The bulges move around the oceans as the Earth rotates, causing high and low tides around the globe.
- The Moon is drifting away from the Earth: The Moon is moving approximately 3.8 cm away from our planet every year. It is estimated that it will continue to do so for around 50 billion years. By the time that happens, the Moon will be taking around 47 days to orbit the Earth instead of the current 27.3 days.
- A person would weigh much less on the Moon: The Moon has much weaker gravity than Earth, due to its smaller mass,

so you would weigh about one sixth (16.5 per cent) of your weight on Earth. This is why the lunar astronauts could leap and bound so high in the air.

- The Moon has no atmosphere: This means that the surface of the Moon is unprotected from cosmic rays, meteorites and solar winds, and has huge temperature variations. The lack of atmosphere means no sound can be heard on the Moon, and the sky always appears black.
- The Moon has quakes: These are caused by the gravitational pull of the Earth. Lunar astronauts used seismographs on their visits to the Moon, and found that small moonquakes occurred several kilometres beneath the surface, causing ruptures and cracks. Scientists think the Moon has a molten core, just like Earth.
- The first spacecraft to reach the Moon was Luna 1 in 1959: This was a Soviet craft, which was launched from the USSR. It passed within 5995 km of the surface of the Moon before going into orbit around the Sun.
- The Moon is the fifth largest natural satellite in the Solar System: At 3,475 km in diametre, the Moon is much smaller than the major moons of Jupiter and Saturn. Earth is about 80 times the volume than the Moon, but both are about the same age. A prevailing theory is that the Moon was once part of the Earth, and was formed from a chunk that broke away due to a huge object colliding with Earth when it was relatively young.
- The Moon will be visited by man in the near future: NASA plans to return astronauts to the moon to set up a permanent space station. Mankind may once again walk on the moon in 2019, if all goes according to plan.
- During the 1950's the USA considered detonating a nuclear bomb on the Moon: The secret project was during the height cold war was known as 'A Study of Lunar Research Flights'.
- The Moon has only been walked on by 12 people; all American males: The first man to set foot on the Moon in 1969 was Neil Armstrong on the Apollo 11 mission, while the last man to walk on the Moon in 1972 was Gene Cernan on the

Apollo 17 mission. Since then the Moon has only be visited by unmanned vehicles. 'Project A119' and meant as a show of strength at a time they were lagging behind in the space race.

Pluto

Discovered in 1930, Pluto is the second closest dwarf planet to the Sun and was at one point classified as the ninth planet. Pluto is the largest dwarf planet but only the second most massive, with Eris being the most massive.

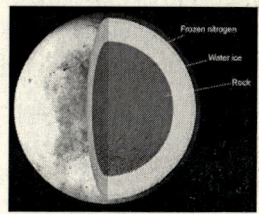

- Pluto is named after the Greek god of the underworld: This is a later name for the more well-known Hades and was proposed by Venetia Burney an eleven year old schoolgirl from Oxford, England.
- Pluto was reclassified from a planet to a dwarf planet in 2006: This is when the IAU formalized the definition of a planet as 'A planet is a celestial body that (a) is in orbit around the Sun, (b) has sufficient mass for its self-gravity to overcome rigid body forces so that it assumes a hydrostatic equilibrium (nearly round) shape, and (c) has cleared the neighbourhood around its orbit.'
- Pluto was discovered on February 18th, 1930 by the Lowell Observatory: For the 76 years between Pluto being discovered and the time it was reclassified as a dwarf planet it completed under a third of its orbit around the Sun.
- Pluto has five known moons: The moons are Charon (discovered in 1978,), Hydra and Nix (both discovered in 2005), Kerberos originally P4 (discovered 2011) and Styx originally P5 (discovered 2012) official designations S/2011 (134340) 1 and S/2012 (134340) 1.
- Pluto is the largest dwarf planet: At one point it was thought this could be Eris. Currently the most accurate measurements give Eris an average diameter of 2,326 km with a margin of error of 12 km, while Pluto's diameter is 2,372 km with a 2 km margin of error.

- Pluto is one third water: This is in the form of water ice which is more than 3 times as much water as in all the Earth's oceans, the remaining two thirds are rock. Pluto's surface is covered with ices, and has several mountain ranges, light and dark regions, and a scattering of craters.
- Pluto is smaller than a number of moons: These are Ganymede, Titan, Callisto, Io, Europa, Triton, and the Earth's moon. Pluto has 66 per cent of the diameter of the Earth's moon and 18 per cent of its mass. While it is now confirmed that Pluto is the largest dwarf planet for around 10 years it was thought that this was Eris.
- Pluto has an eccentric and inclined orbit: This takes it between 4.4 and 7.3 billion km from the Sun meaning Pluto is periodically closer to the Sun than Neptune.

The Milky Way Galaxy

The Milky Way Galaxy is our home galaxy in the universe. It is a fairly typical barred spiral with four major arms in its disk, at least one spur, and a newly discovered outer arm. The galactic centre, which is located about 26,000 light-years from Earth, contains at least one supermassive black hole (called Sagittarius A*), and is crossed by a bar. The Milky Way began forming around 12 billion years ago and is part of a group of about 50 galaxies called the Local Group. The Andromeda Galaxy is part of this group as are numerous smaller galaxies, including the Magellanic Clouds. The Local Group itself is part of a larger gathering of galaxies called the Virgo Supercluster of galaxies.

- The Milky Way began as a series of dense regions in the early universe not long after the Big Bang. The first stars to form were in globular clusters that still exist. They are among the oldest stars formed in the Milky Way region.
- The Milky Way has grown by merging with other galaxies

- through time. It is currently acquiring stars from a very small galaxy called the Sagittarius Dwarf Spheroidal, as well as gobbling up material from the Magellanic Clouds.
- The Milky Way moves through space at a velocity of about 552 kilometres per second (343 miles per second) with respect to the Cosmic Microwave Background radiation.
- The Milky Way's central core contains a supermassive black hole. It is commonly referred to as Sagittarius A. It contains the mass of about 2.6 million Suns.
- The stars, gas and dust of the Milky Way all orbit the centre at a rate of about 220 kilometres per second. This constant rate for all stars at different distances from the core implies the existence of a shell of dark matter surrounding our galaxy.
- Our galaxy will collide with Andromeda Galaxy in about 5 billion years. Some astronomers refer to our two galaxy as a binary system of giant spirals.
- Andromeda Galaxy Facts: The Andromeda Galaxy (M31) is the closest large galaxy to the Milky Way and is one of a few galaxies that can be seen.
- Black Hole Facts: Black holes are among the strangest things in the universe. They are massive objects—collections of mass—with extremely strong gravity.
- M87 Galaxy Facts: The massive galaxy M87 is the most spectacular example of an elliptical galaxy we can see from Earth.

The Andromeda Galaxy

The Andromeda Galaxy (M31) is the closest large galaxy to the Milky Way and is one of a few galaxies that can be seen unaided from the Earth.

In approximately 4.5 billion years the Andromeda Galaxy and the Milky Way are expected to collide and the result will be a giant elliptical galaxy. Andromeda is accompanied by 14 dwarf galaxies, including M32, M110, and possibly M33 (The Triangulum Galaxy).

- While Andromeda is the largest galaxy in the Local Cluster it may not be the most massive. The Milky May is thought to contain more dark matter, which could make it much more massive.
- Since it is the nearest spiral galaxy to us, astronomers use the Andromeda Galaxy to understand the origin and evolution of such galaxies.
- The Andromeda Galaxy is approaching the Milky Way at approximately 100 to 140 kilometres per second.
- The Andromeda Galaxy has a very crowded double nucleus. Not only does it have a massive star cluster right at its heart, but it also has at least one supermassive black hole hidden at the core.
- The spiral arms of the Andromeda Galaxy are being distorted by gravitational interactions with two companion galaxies, M32 and M110.
- The Andromeda Galaxy has at least two spiral arms, plus a ring of dust that may have come from the smaller galaxy M32. Astronomers think that it may have interacted more closely with Andromeda several hundred million years ago, when M32 plunged through the heart of its larger neighbour.
- There are at least 450 globular clusters orbiting in and around the Andromeda Galaxy. Some of them are among the most densely populated globulars ever seen.
- The Andromeda Galaxy is the most distant object you can spot with the naked eye. You need a good spot away from bright lights in order to see it.

Similar Facts

- Triangulum Galaxy Facts: The Triangulum Galaxy, also known as M33, is one of the closest spiral galaxies to the Milky Way. It lies 3 million light-years away.

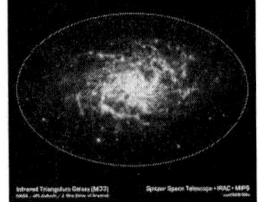

- Antennae Galaxies Facts: The

Antennae is a pair of spiral galaxies that are interacting and mingling their stars.
- Sombrero Galaxy Facts: The Sombrero Galaxy is one of the most unusual looking barred spiral galaxies visible from Earth.

Asteroid Belt

- Asteroid Belt objects are made of rock and stone. Some are solid objects, while others are orbiting 'rubble piles'.

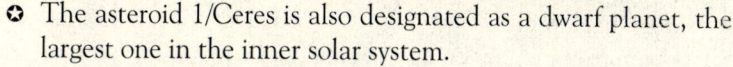

- The Asteroid Belt contains billions and billions of asteroids.
- Some asteroids in the Belt are quite large, but most range in size down to pebbles.
- The asteroid 1/Ceres is also designated as a dwarf planet, the largest one in the inner solar system.
- We know of at least 7,000 asteroids.
- The Asteroid Belt may contain many objects, but they are spread out over a huge area of space. This has allowed spacecraft to move through this region without hitting anything.
- Asteroids get their names from suggestions by their discoverers and are also given a number.
- The formation of Jupiter disrupted the formation of any worlds in the Asteroid Belt region by scattering asteroids away. This caused them to collide and break into smaller pieces.
- Gravitational influences can move asteroids out of the Belt.
- The Asteroid Belt is often referred to as the 'Main Belt' to distinguish it from other groups of asteroids such as the Lagrangians and Centaurs.

Comet Facts

A comet is a very small solar system body made mostly of ices mixed with smaller amounts of dust and rock. Most comets are no larger than *a few kilometres across. The main body of the comet is called the nucleus, and it can contain water, methane, nitrogen and other ices.*

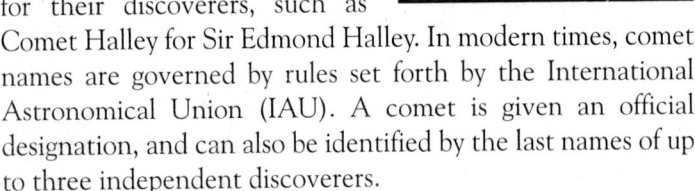

- Comets come in several categories. The most common are periodic and non–periodic.
- In the past, comets were named for their discoverers, such as Comet Halley for Sir Edmond Halley. In modern times, comet names are governed by rules set forth by the International Astronomical Union (IAU). A comet is given an official designation, and can also be identified by the last names of up to three independent discoverers.
- This is how it works: Once a comet has been confirmed, the following naming rules are followed. First, if the comet is a periodic comet, then it is indicated with a P/ followed by the year of its discovery, a letter indicating the half–month in which it was discovered, followed by a number indicating its order of discovery. So, for example, the second periodic comet found in the first half of January, 2015 would be called P/2015 A2.
- A non-periodic comet would be indicated with a C/ followed by the year of its discovery, a letter indicating the half–month in which it was discovered, followed by a number indicating its order of discovery. If a comet is independently discovered by three people named Smith, Jones, and Petersen, it could also be called Comet Smith–Jones–Petersen, in addition to its formal designation. Today, many comets are found through automated instrument searches, and so the formal designations are more commonly used.
- There are many misconceptions about comets, which are simply pieces of solar system ices travelling in orbit around the Sun. Here are some fascinating and true facts about comets.
- The nucleus of a comet is made of ice and can be as small as a few metres across to giant boulders a few kilometres across.

- The closest point in a comet's orbit to the Sun is called 'perihelion'. The most distant point is called 'aphelion'.
- As a comet gets closer to the Sun, it begins to experience heat. That causes some of its ices to sublimate (similar to dry ice sizzling in sunlight). If the ice is close to the comet's surface, it may form a small 'jet' of material spewing out from the comet like a mini-geyser.
- Material streams from comets and populates the comet's orbit. If Earth (or another planet) happens to move through that stream, those particles fall to Earth as meteor showers.
- As a comet gets close to the Sun, it loses some of its mass due to the sublimation. If a comet goes around enough times, it will eventually break up. Comets also break up if they come too close to the Sun or another planet in their orbits.
- Comets are usually made of frozen water and supercold methane, ammonia and carbon dioxide ices. Those are mixed with rock, dust, and other metallic bits of solar system debris. Comets have two tails: a dust tail (which you can see with the naked eye) and a plasma tail, which is easily photographed but difficult to see with your eyes.
- Comet orbits are usually elliptical.
- Many comets formed in the Oort Cloud and Kuiper Belts, two of the outermost regions of the solar system.
- Comets are not spaceships or alien bases. They are fascinating bits of solar system material that date back to the formation of the Sun and planets.

2 Water World

Water Around Us

- Sound moves four times faster than in air.
- More than three-quarters of the human body is made from water, so we can't live without it.
- Just like the rest of our body, our brain is mostly made of water.
- Tears do not look like raindrops although artists do so with their painting skills. They are more sphere-shaped, and large drops are shaped like hamburger buns.
- More than 500,000 of water crash down the 18 story-tall water fall every second.
- Water boils at 212 degree, except at high altitudes, where the boiling point is lower.
- There are plateaus and volcanoes underwater, too. We cannot see it, but there are tiny water molecules in the air we breathe.
- There are two kinds of water; salt water and freshwater. Salt water contains great amounts of salt, whereas freshwater has a dissolved salt concentration of less than 1 per cent. Only freshwater can be applied as drinking water.
- Freshwater fish absorb water, while ocean fish must drink water to keep from getting dehydrated.
- Most of the Earth's water is either salt water or ice.

- There is the same amount of water on earth as there was when the earth was formed.
- The overall amount of water on our planet has remained the same for two billion years.
- Water moves around the earth in a water cycle. The water cycle has five parts: evaporation, condensation, precipitation, infiltration and surface run-off.

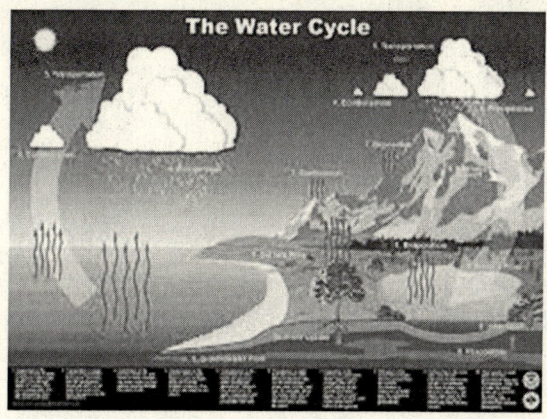

- In a 100-year period, a water molecule spends 98 years in the ocean, 20 months as ice, about 2 weeks in lakes and rivers, and less than a week in the atmosphere.
- Most of the earth's surface water is permanently frozen or salty.
- Water regulates the earth's temperature.
- Water is the only substance that is found naturally on earth in three forms: liquid, gas, solid.
- Frozen water is 9 per cent lighter than water, which is why ice floats on water.
- A litre of water weighs 1.01 kilograms.
- It doesn't take much salt to make water 'salty'. If one-thousandth (or more) of the weight of water is from salt, then the water is 'saline'.
- Saline water can be desalinated for use as drinking water by going through a process to remove the salt from the water.

- When water contains a lot of calcium and magnesium, it is called hard water. Hard water is not suited for all purposes water is normally used for.
- If all the water of the world were fit into a gallon jug, the fresh water available for us to use would equal only about one tablespoon.
- Over 90 per cent of the world's supply of fresh water is located in Antarctica.
- Less than 1 per cent of the water supply on earth can be used as drinking water.
- The earth's total amount of water has a volume of about 344 million cubic miles.
- 315 million cubic miles is seawater.
- Human bones are 25 per cent water.
- Human blood is 83 per cent water.
- 75 per cent of a chicken is water.
- 80 per cent of a pineapple is water.
- 95 per cent of a tomato is water.
- Each day the sun evaporates a trillion tons of water.
- A small drip from a water tap can waste as much as 75 litres of water a day.
- Humans use more and more water each year.
- Two thirds of the water used in a home is used in the bathroom.
- To flush a toilet we use 7.5 to 26.5 litres (2 to 7 gallons) of water.
- In a five-minute shower we use 95 to 190 litres (25 to 50 gallons) of water.
- To brush your teeth you use 7.5 litres (2 gallons) of water.

> **INSIDE OUT**
>
> It can take up to 2,000 gallons of water to produce one gallon of milk. The cow needs water to perform basic biological functions from day to day, and only a fraction of the water the cow consumes is actually converted into milk.

Oceans

- 94 percent of life on Earth is aquatic. That makes us land-dwellers a very small minority.
- About 70 percent of the planet is ocean, with an average depth of more than 12,400 feet.
- Fifty per cent of the United States (in terms of our complete legal jurisdiction, which includes ocean territory) lies below the ocean.
- The deep sea is the largest museum on Earth: There are more artifacts and remnants of history in the ocean than in all of the world's museums, combined.
- We have only explored less than 5 percent of the Earth's oceans. In fact, we have better maps of Mars than we do of the ocean floor!
- The longest mountain range in the world is under water. Called the Mid-Oceanic Ridge, this chain of mountains runs through the middle of the Atlantic Ocean and into the Indian and Pacific oceans.
- We didn't send divers down to explore the Mid-Ocean Ridge until 1973—four years after Neil Armstrong and Buzz Aldrin walked on the moon—when a French–American crew of seven entered the 9,000-foot-deep Great Rift in the French submersible Archimede.
- An estimated 50–80 per cent of all life on earth is found under the ocean surface.
- The oceans contain 99 per cent of the living space on the planet. Less than 10 per cent of that space has been explored by humans. 85 per cent of the area and 90 per cent of the volume constitute the dark, cold environment we call the deep sea.
- The oceans cover 71 per cent (and rising) of the Earth's surface and contain 97 per cent of the Earth's water. Less than 1 per

cent is fresh water, and 2–3 per cent is contained in glaciers and ice caps (and is decreasing).
- 90 per cent of all volcanic activity occurs in the oceans.
- The highest tides in the world are at the Bay of Fundy, which separates New Brunswick from Nova Scotia.
- The top ten feet of the ocean holds as much heat as the entire atmosphere.
- The lowest known point on Earth, called the *Challenger Deep*.
- Undersea earthquakes, volcanoes and landslides can cause tsunamis (Japanese word meaning 'harbor wave'), or seismic sea waves.
- The average depth of the Atlantic Ocean, with its adjacent seas, is 3,332 m; without them it is 3,926 m.
- The Pacific Ocean, the world's largest water body, occupies a third of the Earth's surface.
- The Pacific contains about 25,000 islands (more than the total number in the rest of the world's oceans combined), almost all of which are found south of the equator.
- The Kuroshio Current, off the shores of Japan, is the largest current.
- A given area in an ocean upwelling zone or deep estuary is as productive as the same area in rain forests, most crops and intensive agriculture.
- The sea level has risen over the past 100 years and scientists expect this rate to increase. Sea levels will continue rising even if the climate has stabilized, because the ocean reacts slowly to changes.
- Antarctica has as much ice as the Atlantic Ocean has water.
- The Arctic produces 10,000–50,000 icebergs annually. Icebergs normally have a four-year life-span; they begin entering shipping lanes after about three years.
- Air pollution is responsible for 33 per cent of the toxic contaminants that end up in oceans and coastal waters.
- Each year, three times, as much rubbish, is dumped into the world's oceans as the weight of fish caught.
- Oil is one of the ocean's 'greatest' resources. Nearly one-third of the world's oil comes from offshore fields in our oceans.

- Areas most popular for oil drilling are the Arabian Gulf, the North Sea and the Gulf of Mexico.
- Refined oil is also responsible for polluting the ocean. More oil reaches the oceans each year as a result of leaking automobiles and other non-point sources than the oil spilled.
- A mouthful of seawater may contain millions of bacterial cells, hundreds of thousands of phytoplankton and tens of thousands of zooplankton.
- Fish supply the greatest percentage of the world's protein consumed by humans and most of the world's major fisheries are being fished at levels above their maximum sustainable yield; some regions are severely overfished.
- More than 90 per cent of the trade between countries is carried by ships and about half the communications between nations use underwater cables.
- Swordfish and marlin are the fastest fish in the ocean.
- Blue whales are the largest animals on our planet ever (exceeding the size of the greatest known dinosaurs) and have hearts the size of small cars.
- Oarfish are the longest bony fish in the world. They have a snakelike body sporting a magnificent red fin.
- Many fish can change sex during the course of their lives. Others, especially rare deep-sea fish, have both male and female sex organs.

INSIDE OUT

The United Nations has declared June 8, as World Oceans Day. The concept of a 'World Ocean Day' was first proposed in 1992 by the Government of Canada at the Earth Summit in Rio de Janeiro.

Sea World

- The oceans are filled with both marvels and mysteries.
- Earth's oceans contain approximately 324 million cubic miles of seawater. It is also believed that the earth's oceans formed over four billion years ago.
- Nautiluses, like many sea creatures, rely on a combination of carbon and oxygen in the seawater to form their shells.
- The Pacific Ocean is the earth's largest covering 70,000,000 square miles. It was named by explorer Ferdinand Magellan.
- Around 70 per cent of the Earth's surface is covered by oceans.
- The world's oceans contain enough water to fill a cube with edges over 1000 kilometres (621 miles) in length.
- The largest ocean on Earth is the Pacific Ocean, it covers around 30 per cent of the Earth's surface.
- The Pacific Ocean's name has an original meaning of 'peaceful sea'.
- Located to the east of the Mariana Islands in the western Pacific Ocean, the Mariana Trench is the deepest known area of Earth's oceans. It has a deepest point of around 11000 metres (36000 feet).
- The Pacific Ocean contains around 25000 different islands, many more than are found in Earth's other oceans.
- The Pacific Ocean is surrounded by the Pacific Ring of Fire, a large number of active volcanoes.
- The second largest ocean on Earth is the Atlantic Ocean, it covers over 21 per cent of the Earth's surface.
- The Atlantic Ocean's name refers to Atlas of Greek mythology.
- The Bermuda Triangle is located in the Atlantic Ocean.
- Amelia Earhart became the first female to fly solo across the Atlantic Ocean in 1932.
- The third largest ocean on Earth is the Indian Ocean; it covers around 14 per cent of the Earth's surface.
- During winter the Arctic Ocean is almost completely covered in sea ice.

- Ocean tides are caused by the Earth rotating while the Moon and Sun's gravitational pull acts on ocean water.
- While there are hundreds of thousands of known marine life forms, there are many that are yet to be discovered, some scientists suggest that there could actually be millions of marine life forms out there.
- Oceans are frequently used as a means of transport with various companies shipping their products across oceans from one port to another.
- Polar bears can remain completely submerged underwater for about two minutes. They close their nostrils but they swim with their eyes open.
- Coorong Lagoon off the southern coast of Australia is a famous haven for birds such as pelicans and swans.
- Mangrove swamps cover approximately eight percent of the earth's coastlines. However, in recent decades, half have been destroyed due to human enterprise.
- The largest continual mangrove ecosystem in the world is the Sundarbans Mangrove Forest located in southwestern Bangladesh and northeastern India.
- A fast-grower, giant kelp, the ocean's biggest seaweed, can grow about twenty inches per day.
- Among a few threatened marine species of the Indian Ocean are whales, turtles, seals and dugongs—relatives of manatees.
- Global warming trends currently threaten animals like polar bears but also cities like Venice, which floods about two hundred times a year.
- The Skeleton Coast off the northwestern coast of Namibia is the scene of many historical shipwrecks due to rough seas, fog and high winds.
- Puget Sound off the Pacific coast of North America was formed by glaciers roughly 20,000 years ago.
- The lowest point in the Pacific Ocean is *Challenger Deep* in the Mariana Trench.
- The deepest point in the Atlantic Ocean is the Puerto Rico Trench.

- Estuary surfing is popular in countries like Brazil, but dangerous as these waters are often teeming with snakes and crocodiles.
- The earthquake of 2004 that launched the horrific Indian Ocean Tsunami produced 23,000 more energy than the atomic bomb dropped on Hiroshima.
- One of the most dangerous sea creatures is the blue octopus. Its neurotoxic venom can kill a human being.
- Moray eels are nocturnal creatures that live in coral reefs.
- The sea horse is the only creature where the male gets to deal with pregnancy. Although the female produces the eggs, the father holds them within his body until their births.
- Benjamin Franklin made one of the earliest maps of the Gulf Stream's course.
- Tornadoes that whirl over the sea are actually called waterspouts and are frequently caused by tropical cyclones.
- Daily tides are cause by the gravitational exchange between the earth and moon.
- There are many known whirlpools throughout the oceans. The Naruto Whirlpool between two islands of Japan has been in existence since ancient times.
- Starfish are actually carnivores eating small fish, clams and oysters.
- The biggest great white shark recorded weighed in at seven thousand pounds.
- At any given time, great whites smile with approximately three thousand teeth.
- Bull sharks are referred to by many different names such as: Ganges shark, river shark, shovelnose shark and the Zambezi shark.
- A tablespoon of seawater contains a few organisms or bacteria.
- One-fourth of the people of this world rely on the oceans for its main source of protein.
- Humans have explored more than 90 per cent of the world's oceans.

- The world's longest mountain range lies on the ocean floor.
- At least one creature living in the sea has blue blood.
- There's gold to be found in the ocean.
- About 40 per cent of Earth's volcanic activity happens in the oceans.
- During the summer, the Arctic Ocean is almost covered by ice.
- Scientists are looking for organisms on the ocean floor to make into cancer medicine.
- Scientists currently have named about 200,000 marine species.
- The levels of the oceans have been rising for more than a century.
- Most of the ocean's heat is in the top 10 feet of water.
- There are 25,000 islands in the Pacific Ocean.
- Earthquakes under the sea can cause hurricanes to form.
- More oil is drilled in the Mediterranean se than anywhere else in the world.
- The colossal squid, the world's largest squid, is longer than a school bus.
- Humans have explored more than 90 percent of the world's oceans.
- An octopus has four hearts.
- A blue whale's heart is about the size of a house.
- Orcas, also called killer whales, belong to the dolphin family.

- The water pressure in the deepest part of the world's oceans is equivalent the weight of 50 jet planes on the shoulders of one person.
- The Atlantic Ocean is the world's largest ocean.
- One-fourth of the world's population relies on the oceans for its main source of protein.
- The fastest shark is the mako.
- The world's longest mountain range lies on the ocean floor.
- A tablespoon of seawater contains only a few organisms or bacteria.

- Sound travels more slowly through water than it does through air.
- There's gold to be found in the ocean.
- At least one creature living in the sea has blue blood.
- About 40 percent of earth's volcanic activity happens in the oceans.
- Scientists currently have named about 200,000 marine species.
- Most of the ocean's heat is in the top 10 feet (3m) of water.
- Earthquakes under the sea can cause hurricanes to form.
- The levels of ocean water have been rising for more than a century.
- The Atlantic Ocean gets its name from an ancient Greek myth.
- There are about 25,000 islands in the Pacific Ocean.
- More oil is drilled in the Mediterranean sea than anywhere else on earth.
- Blue whales living in the oceans today are larger than any dinosaur known to have lived.
- The gray whale migrates 10,000 miles (16,100 km) each year.
- The oceans' tides are affected by the gravitational pull between earth and the moon.
- Scientists are looking for organisms on the ocean floor to make into cancer medicine.
- During the summer, the Arctic Ocean is almost totally covered by ice.
- Coral is so similar to human bone that doctors have used it in operations to repair bones.

> **INSIDE OUT**
> The word 'scuba' comes from the phrase 'solo continuous undersea bathing apparatus'.

River Talk

- Small rivers often have different names which include creek, stream and brook.
- Rivers normally contain freshwater.
- The word upriver (or upstream) refers to the direction of the river's water source, while downriver (or downstream) refers to the direction in which the water flows, i.e. towards the end of the river.
- Rivers have many uses which include fishing, bathing, transport, rafting and swimming among others.
- Most of the world's major cities are located near the banks of rivers.
- The Congo River is in Africa is the deepest river in the world.

- The bottom of a river is called the Sole, like the sole of a shoe.
- The Mekong river runs through 6 countries—China, Burma, Vietnam, Laos, Cambodia and Thailand.
- The Dead Sea is not a sea. It is a lake between Israel and Jordan.
- People in Russia tiptoe along rivers so that they do not disturb fish laying eggs.
- The Great Salt Lake in Utah actually has fresh water.
- A waterfall can never freeze.
- The Nile River is called 'The Cradle of Civilization'.
- The Yellow River in China is considered to be the world's cleanest river.
- The longest river in the world is the Nile River; it reaches around 6650 kilometres in length (4132 miles).
- The second longest river in the world is the Amazon River; it reaches around 4000 miles in length.
- The longest river in the USA is the Missouri River, stretching around 2,340 miles in length (slightly longer than the Mississippi River). The two combine to form the longest river system in

North America, reaching around 3902 miles in length.
- The Ganges, Yangtze and Indus rivers are three of the most polluted on Earth.
- The world's third longest river, the Yangtze, dumps an average of 7.9 million gallons of water per second into the East China Sea.
- The Colorado River travels through the southwestern United States and northwestern Mexico, it is home to the famous Hoover Dam.

> **INSIDE OUT**
>
> The Helmand River is the longest river in Afghanistan. It flows for 1,150 km (710 miles) and rises approximately 80 km (50 miles) west of Kabul.

Barrier Reef

- The reef is a conglomerate of 2900 coral reefs and 1050 islands and cays.
- The 1,430-mile long Great Barrier Reef can fit inside the US state of Alaska.
- The Great Barrier Reef is an extremely ancient, enormous host of living things, composed of living coral growing on dead coral dating back perhaps as much as twenty million years.
- The Great Barrier Reef is a popular tourist destination with over two million visitors each year.
- Tourism to the reef generates approximately AU$5-6 billion per year.
- The Great Barrier Reef is greater in size than the United Kingdom, Holland and Switzerland combined.
- The Great Barrier Reef is approximately the same area as Italy, Germany, Malaysia or Japan.
- The Great Barrier Reef is roughly half the size of Texas.

- The Great Barrier Reef is a great holiday destination for families and kids.
- The Great Barrier Reef is the world's largest reef system.
- The Great Barrier Reef is composed of over 2,900 individual reef.
- The Great Barrier Reef has over 900 islands stretching for over 2,600 kilometres.
- The Great Barrier Reef can be seen from outer space.
- The Great Barrier Reef is greater in size than Tasmania and Victoria combined.
- Thirty species of whales, dolphins, and porpoises have been recorded in the Great Barrier Reef.
- Six species of sea turtles come to the reef to breed.
- 215 species of birds (including 22 species of seabirds and 32 species of shorebirds) visit the reef or nest or roost on the islands.
- Seventeen species of sea snake live on the Great Barrier Reef.
- More than 1,500 fish species live on the reef.
- Around 10 percent of the world's total fish species can be found just within the Great Barrier Reef.
- There are at least 330 species of ascidians on the reef system.
- Climate change is perhaps the biggest threat to the Great Barrier Reef.
- Warmer ocean temperatures put stress on coral and lead to coral bleaching.
- The Great Barrier Reef has experienced two mass coral bleaching events in 1998 and 2002.
- Bleaching was more severe in 2002, when aerial surveys showed that over 50 per cent of reefs experienced some coral bleaching.
- Coral is alive, made up of many small, soft-bodied creatures called polyps.
- From Space, the Great Barrier Reef looks like a light blue line off the coast of Australia.
- Corals eat algae.
- Spinefoot fish lives in the Great Barrier Reef.

> **INSIDE OUT**
>
> The Great Barrier Reef is approximately 350,000 square kilometres in size and stretches 2300 kilometres along the coastline of Queensland—that's the size of about 70 million football fields. And of course, it is the only living structure in the world that can be seen from space.

World Rivers

- Nile (Africa): 4,132 miles
- Amazon (South America): 4,087 miles
- Yangtze (Asia): 3,915 miles
- Huang He, aka Yellow (Asia): 3,395 miles
- Parana (South America): 3,032 miles
- Congo (Africa): 2,900 miles
- Amur (Asia): 2,761 miles
- Lena (Asia): 2,734 miles
- Mekong (Asia): 2,700 miles
- Mackenzie (Canada): 2,635 miles
- Niger (Africa): 2,600 miles
- Yenisey (Russia): 2,543 miles
- Missouri (United States): 2,540 miles
- Mississippi (United States): 2,340 miles
- Ob (Russia): 2,268 miles
- Zambezi (Africa): 2,200 miles
- Volga (Europe): 2,193 miles
- Purus (Brazil): 1,995 miles
- Yukon (United States/Canada): 1,980 miles
- Rio Grande (United States/Mexico): 1,900 miles
- St. Lawrence (United States/Canada): 1,900 miles
- Sao Francisco (Brazil): 1,811 miles
- Brahmaputra (India): 1,800 miles
- Indus (India): 1,800 miles
- Danube (Europe): 1,770 miles

More to know

Deepest Spot in the Ocean
The deepest spot in the ocean is called the Mariana Trench and is approximately 35, 797 ft (10,911 m) deep in the Pacific Ocean. That's deeper than the height of the world's highest mountain, Mount Everest, which is 29,035 ft (8,850 m) high.

Highest Navigable Lake
Lake Titicaca in Peru is the highest navigable lake in the world. It is about 12,500 ft (3,810 m) above sea level. This lake is also South America's second largest freshwater lake.

Lowest Lake
The lowest lake is the Dead Sea (it's considered a lake but called a sea), which is in the Jordan Valley of Israel. The surface of the water is 1,340 ft (408 m) below sea level. The Dead Sea is also the saltiest lake in the world. Almost nothing can survive in it besides simple organisms like green algae.

Largest Freshwater Lake
Lake Superior is the largest of the Great Lakes and it's also the freshwater lake that covers the greatest surface area in the world. Lake Superior covers over 82,000 km of land and there's enough water in the lake to fill all the other Great Lakes plus three Lake Eries.

Deepest Lake
Lake Baikal is the world's deepest lake and is located in Siberia, Russia, north of the Mongolian border. It is 5,369 ft (1,637 m) deep—more than one mile straight down.

Largest Ocean
The Pacific Ocean takes the award for being the largest ocean in the world. It covers almost a third of the Earth's surface and goes from the Bering Sea in the Arctic north to the icy waters of Antarctica's Ross Sea in the south.

Smallest Ocean

The smallest ocean is the Arctic Ocean, which is about 10 times smaller than the Pacific Ocean.

Longest River

The Nile River in Egypt is the longest river. It's 4,145 miles (6,671 km) long and flows into the Mediterranean Sea.

Shortest River

The world's shortest river, according to the Guinness Book of World Records, is the Roe River. It is only 200 feet (61 meters) long and flows between Giant Springs and the Missouri River near Great Falls, Montana. There has been debate, though, about which river is really the shortest. The D River in Oregon has been measured as being only 120 ft (37 m) long. It connects Devil's Lake directly to the Pacific Ocean near Lincoln City. Because the D River flows into the ocean though, it's length changes according to the tide so has been measured at several different lengths.

Largest River

The Amazon Basin in South America is the largest river with the greatest water flow. This is because it flows through the Amazon rain forest—the largest and wettest rainforest on Earth.

Highest Waterfall

Angel Falls (Salto Angel) in Canaima National Park, Venezuela is the highest waterfall in the world at 3212 ft (979 m).

Scared Rivers of India

The rivers of India are the main source of living of the Indian people. There are some major Rivers in India like Ganga, Yamuna, Narmada, Mahanadi and Brahmaputra. Punjab, the land of five great rivers—Jhelum, Chenab, Ravi, Beas

and Sutlej. Every river of Punjab has its own significance and symbolic importance. The seven rivers are counted as the holy rivers of India, one of the most holiest river in India is Ganga or The Ganges. Rivers are India's lifeline and enjoy a special place in prayers and its traditional practices. Most of the holy places in India like, Varanasi, Haridwar, Talakaveri, Nasik, Ujjain and Patna are situated along with the bank of seven holy rivers. The Triveni Sangam in Allahabad is a confluence of 3 rivers—the Ganges, Yamuna, and the mythological Saraswati river. A place of religious importance and the site for historic Kumbh Mela held every 12 years and Sadhus, the holy men of India gather here for holy bath from all over India. It is said that by taking a bath in the holy rivers, man can be freed from all the sins of his life. Apart from the rivers the Hindu also worship trees, stones and animals, they believed that they are the forms of different deities.

Ganga River

The Ganges, originates in the Himalayas at Gaumukh flowing into the Bay of Bengal is the most sacred river of India and the longest river in India. The river has been declared as India's 'National River' and the Ganga dolphins are also declared as the national aquatic animal of India. There are so many tributary to the Ganga like Yamuna, Chambal, Betwa and one of the major is the Ghaghara, which meets it before Patna. Varanasi is one of the oldest continuously inhabited cities in the world, it has has hundreds of temples so called 'City of Temples' is situated along the banks of the Ganges. There are two major dams in the Ganges river one is The Haridwar dam and another is Farakka. One of the longest road bridge in India named Mahatma Gandhi Setu is built on river Ganga at Patna. The mouth of River Ganga forms a vast delta, the Sundarban delta, the largest delta in the world, Also these rivers create some of the beautiful valleys in India.

Yamuna River

Yamuna River is a major river and most polluted river of the Indian subcontinent, rising from Yamunotri in the Himalaya Mountains and merges with the Ganges at Triveni Sangam, Allahabad, the site for the Kumbha Mela. This is one of the country's most sacred rivers, Gokul and Mathura on the other bank of the river are holy places for hindu. The Tons, Chambal and Giri rivers are the important tributaries of Yamuna, River Mandakini is the last tributaries of river Yamuna before it joins the Ganga in Allahabad. The famous Taj Mahal is situated on the bank of the holy Hindu river Yamuna in Agra. One of the famous Naini Bridge stands across the Yamuna river.

Saraswati River

Saraswati is an ancient river that flowed in northern India during the Vedic era. Although the river does not have a physical existence today, the ancient river was lost in the desert. The Triveni Sangam in Allahabad is a confluence of 3 rivers—the Ganges, Yamuna, and Saraswati. Of these three, the legendary Saraswati River is invisible and is said to flow underground and join the other two rivers from below and the point of confluence is a sacred place for Hindus.

Narmada River

The Narmada is one of the most sacred of the seven holy rivers of India. Narmada River originates from the Maikala ranges at Amarkantak in Madhya Pradesh and flows between the Vindhya and Satpura ranges in a generally southwestern direction and emptying into the Gulf of Khambhat or Gulf of Cambay, an inlet of the Arabian Sea. The Narmada valley has many waterfalls, Dhuandhar waterfall and deepest waterfall Kapiladhara are best. Sardar Sarover dam one of the India's known dam projects was built across the Narmada river. Narmada Bridge is the Longest Road Bridge in Gujarat. Narmada River is one of only three major rivers in peninsular India that runs from east to west along with the Tapti River and Mahi River. The Hindu God, Lord Shiva Omkareshwar temple on the banks of Narmada river situated in the Khandwa district of Madhya Pradesh; also this district host India's largest water reservoir known as Indira Sagar.

Kshipra River

The Shipra, also known as the Kshipra rises in the Vindhya Range north of Dhar and flows south across the Malwa Plateau to join the Chambal River. It is one of the sacred rivers in Hinduism. The holy city Ujjain is situated on its right bank. Ujjain is an ancient city of Malwa region in central India and famous for one of the twelve celebrated Jyotirlingas in India known as Mahakaleshwar. In every 12 years, the Kumbh Mela festival takes place on the city and millions of people take holy dip and bath in the holy river Shipra.

Godavari River

The river Godavari originates near Trimbak in Nashik flows towards the Eastern Ghats into the Bay of Bengal. This second largest river is considered to be one of the big river basins in India. Kumbh Mela at Nashik is well known as an important center of Pilgrimage in India because the holy river Godavari. Godavari, the largest and the longest river of South India is popularly referred as to as the Dakshina Ganga. Jayakwadi dam is one of the largest earthen dams in India build across Godavari River in Maharashtra.

Kaveri River

Kaveri or Cauvery River is considered to be a very sacred river of southern India. It originates from the Brahmagiri Hill in the Western Ghats flow towards the Bay of Bengal. This sacred river travels across the heartland of Karnataka and Tamil Nadu. It is one of the major rivers of the Peninsular flowing east and running into the Bay of Bengal. The Mettur Dam is a large dam built across the Kaveri River. The beautiful Shivasamudram falls of Kaveri river is the second biggest water falls in India.

Major Rivers

The rivers of India play an important role in the lives of the Indian people. The river systems provide irrigation, potable water, cheap transportation, electricity, as well as provide livelihoods for a large number of people all over the country. This easily explains why nearly all the major cities of India are located by the banks of river. The rivers also have an important role in Hindu mythology and are considered holy by all Hindus in the country.

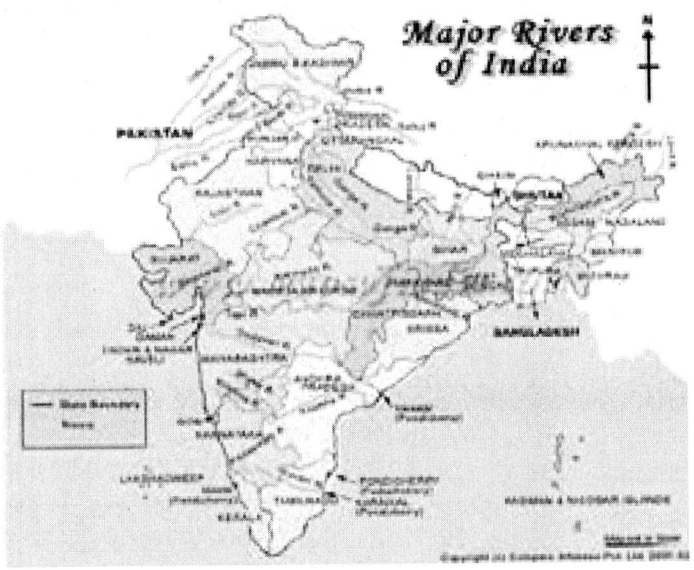

Seven major rivers (Indus, Brahmaputra, Narmada, Tapi, Godavari, Krishna and Mahanadi) along with their numerous tributaries make up the river system of India. Most of the rivers pour their waters into the Bay of Bengal. Some of the rivers whose courses take them through the western part of the country and towards the east of the state of Himachal Pradesh empty into the Arabian Sea. Parts of Ladakh, northern parts of the Aravalli range and the arid parts of the Thar Desert have inland drainage. All major rivers of India originate from one of the three main watersheds:

1. The Himalaya and the Karakoram ranges
2. Vindhya and Satpura ranges and Chotanagpur plateau in central India
3. Sahyadri or Western Ghats in western India

The Himalayan rivers are best for white water sports like rafting and other river sports.

3 The Plant World

- The earth has more than 80,000 species of edible plants.
- 90 per cent of the foods humans eat come from just 30 plants.
- Nutrition doesn't factor into the crops we do mass produce.
- 70,000 plant species are utilised for medicine.
- Only one per cent of rainforest plants have been studied for medicinal potential.
- 80 per cent of the Earth's original forests have been cleared or destroyed.
- Just 10 per cent of the world's plant–rich areas are protected.
- More than half of plant species are native to just one country.
- 68 per cent of plants are in danger of going extinct.
- Plant species are going extinct—about 5,000 times faster than they should.

It isn't strange

- 84 per cent of a raw apple is water.
- 99 per cent of the pumpkins sold in the US end up as jack-o-lanterns.
- A cucumber is 96 per cent water.
- A notch in a tree will remain the same distance from the ground as the tree grows.
- A pineapple is a berry.
- Almonds are the oldest, most widely cultivated and extensively used nuts in the world.
- Americans eat more bananas than any other fruit: a total of 11 billion a year.
- An average ear of corn has 800 kernels, arranged in 16 rows.
- Arrowroot, an antidote for poisoned arrows, is used as a thickener in cooking.
- Avocados have the highest calories of any fruit at 167 calories per hundred grams.
- Banana oil never saw a banana; it's made from petroleum.
- Bananas are actually herbs. Bananas die after fruiting, like all herbs do.
- Both George Washington and Thomas Jefferson grew cannabis sativa (marijuana) on their plantations.
- Cranberries are one of just 3 major fruits native to North America. Blueberries and Concord grapes are the other two.
- Eggplant is a member of the thistle family.
- Ginger has been clinically demonstrated to work twice as well as Dramamine for fighting motion sickness, with no side effects.
- Hydroponics is the technique by which plants are grown in water without soil.
- Nutmeg is extremely poisonous if injected intravenously.
- Oak trees do not have acorns until they are fifty years old or older.
- One pound of tea can make 300 cups of the beverage.
- One ragweed plant can release as many as one billion grains of pollen.

- Oranges, lemons, watermelons, and tomatoes are berries.
- Orchids have the smallest seeds. It takes more than 1.25 million seeds to weigh 1 gram.
- Peanuts are beans.
- Plants that need to attract moths for pollination are generally white or pale yellow, to be better seen when the light is dim.
- Plants that depend on butterflies, such as the poppy or the hibiscus, have more colourful flowers.
- Quinine, one of the most important drugs known to man, is obtained from the dried bark of an evergreen tree native to South America.
- Rice paper isn't made from rice but from a small tree which grows in Taiwan.
- Tea was so expensive when it was first brought to Europe in the early 17th century that it was kept in locked wooden boxes.
- The California redwood—coast redwood and giant sequoia—are the tallest and largest living organism in the world.
- The first American advertisement for tobacco was published in 1789. It showed a picture of an Indian smoking a long clay pipe.
- The fragrance of flowers is due to the essences of oil which they produce.
- The largest single flower is the Rafflesia or 'corpse flower'. They are generally 3 feet in diametre with the record being 42 inches.
- The oldest living thing in existence is not a giant redwood, but a bristlecone pine in the White Mountains of California, dated to be aged 4,600 years old.
- The pineapple was symbol of welcome in the 1700–1800's. That is why in New England you will see so many pineapples on door knockers.
- The plant life in the oceans make about 85 percent of all the greenery on the Earth.
- The popular name for the giant sequoia tree is Redwood.
- The rose family of plants, in addition to flowers, gives us apples, pears, plums, cherries, almonds, peaches and apricots.

- The world's tallest grass, which has sometimes grown 130 feet or more, is bamboo.
- There are more than 700 species of plants that grow in the United States that have been identified as dangerous if eaten. Among them are some that are commonly favored by gardeners: buttercups, daffodils, lily of the valley, sweet peas, oleander, azalea, bleeding heart, delphinium, and rhododendron.
- Willow bark, which provides the salicylic acid from which aspirin was originally synthesized, has been used as a pain remedy ever since the Greeks discovered its therapeutic power nearly 2,500 years ago.

> **INSIDE OUT**
> A rose is a rose: When you give someone roses, the color can have a meaning.
> The meaning of rose colors:
> Red = Love and respect
> Deep pink = Gratitude, appreciation
> Light pink = Admiration, sympathy
> White = Reverence, humility
> Yellow = Joy, gladness
> Orange = Enthusiasm, desire
> Red & yellow blend = Gaiety, joviality
> Pale blended tones = Sociability, friendship

- The spice saffron comes from a certain type of crocus.
- Tulip bulbs can be used in place of onions for cooking.
- In 1986 Congress voted to make the rose America's national flower.
- The bluebonnet became the Texas state flower in 1901. In 1971, the state legislature, named all lupine species as the official state flower.
- Pink and White Lady Slipper (cypripedium reginae) is the State flower of Minnesota. Illegal to pick in the state, the pink and white

- lady slipper is one of Minnesota's rarest wildflowers. They can take up to 16 years to produce their first flower, and sometimes live for 50 years.
- The creamy-white bloom of the magnolia tree was designated the state flower of Louisiana in 1900 because of the abundance of trees throughout the state. Magnolia is an evergreen and the flower is usually fragrant. After the six to twelve petals of the flower have fallen away the large cone shaped fruit of the magnolia is exposed.
- The Peach Blossom became the State flower of Delaware on May 9, 1895. It was prompted by Delaware's reputation as the 'Peach State', since her orchards contained more than 800,000 peach trees yielding a crop worth thousands of dollars at that time.
- California is the source for nearly 60 per cent of all USA-grown fresh cut flowers.
- Americans bought more than 1.2 billion fresh cut roses in the year 1996. That's 4.67 roses for every man, woman and child nationwide.
- The number of Begonia hybrids is estimated between 1000 and 2000. Within this enormous family there are plants which are tiny enough to grow in an egg shell and others which can cover a greenhouse wall. If you become addicted to growing begonias you are called a begoniac.
- The first recorded plant collectors were the soldiers in the army of Thothmes III, Pharaoh of Egypt, 3500 years ago. In the Temple of Karnak these soldiers are shown bringing back 300 plants as booty from Syria.
- In 1990 about 250 ha. were cultivated with orchids in Malaysia, producing over 27.86 million stalks of cutflowers, valued at RM 18.30 million. Exports of orchids were valued at RM 3.4 million in 1991.
- The cactus family is divided into more than 100 genera. For simplicity North American cacti are placed into five groups: the prickly pears, the saguaro cactus group, the hedgehog cacti, the barrel cacti, and the pin-cushion and fishhook cacti.

- In 1890 Luther Burbank crossed oxeye field daisy and Japanese daisy to produce perhaps the quintessential chrysanthemum— The Shasta Daisy.
- The rose of Great Britain was the symbol of the Royal Family. As time passed, it became the national flower.
- The rose of Scotland was a kind of weed called 'the wild thistle'. A long time ago, when Vikings invaded Scotland, they were slowed in their attack by the thorns of the wild thistle. This allowed the people of Scotland time to escape from the Viking's sudden attack. Because of this legend, 'the wild thistle' became the national flower of Scotland.
- The national flower of Wales was a kind of a smelly Leek. When the English sneer at someone, they say 'Eat the Leek'. That is the reason why Wales has changed their national flower to a narcissus.
- Germany's national flower, centaurea is related with the emperor of old Germany. It has been called the 'Emperor's flower'. Because of the authoritative language of the flower's name, it naturally has been considered the national flower. Its status was not changed after the republic of Germany was established.
- Egypt is known as the starting place of the ancient civilisations. The water lily has been Egypt's national flower for about 4000 years. It can be seen anywhere on the river Nile, especially the 'blue water lily'. The blue water lily has been loved by Egyptians for a long time. It was also considered the 'God of the Resurrection', so it is sometimes laid on the tomb of 'Mica'. Most of the Arab countries have followed Egypt's custom of adopting a water lily as the national flower.
- The World's Largest Flower: The Titan Arum is not only the world's largest flower, it is also the world's smelliest.
- This native of the central Sumatran rainforests is known affectionately as the Corpse Flower for its heady perfume of rotting flesh. It is 3 metres high.

- The World's Smallest Flower: A bouquet of a dozen Wolffia blooms would comfortably fit on the head of a pin. This very minute flowering plant is native to Australia and Malaysia. The plant body is 0.6–0.9 mm long and only 0.2–0.5 mm wide. Not only is it one of the smallest flowering plants on earth, but it also produces one of the smallest fruits.
- The World's Largest Bouquet: 70,000 roses went into the making of the world's largest flower bouquet. The 23.4 metre arrangement was the work of Ashrita Furman.

4 Bird Kingdom

There are around 10,000 different species of birds worldwide. All birds are classified as members of the Kindom Animalia, Phylum Chordata and Class Aves. This general grouping emphasizes that birds are related in the other characteristics they share, including:

Vertebrates: All birds have a backbone, which places them in the Phylum Chordata. Unlike most other vertebrates, however, birds have a lighter skeletal structure filled with hollows and air sacs to keep them lightweight.

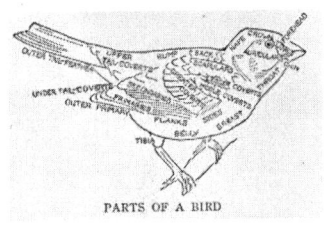

PARTS OF A BIRD

Feathers: All birds have evolved feathers, composed of keratin and other proteins and light-reflecting pigments, to serve as body insulation. Different types of feathers may also be ornamental, such as plumes, while other feather types help birds control their flight.

Wings: Wings are one of the most defining characteristics of birds, and even flightless birds have vestigial or adapted wings they may use for swimming, threat displays or courtship dances. The size and shape of wings varies between species based on how the bird flies, and wing markings are useful to identify bird species.

Bill: All birds have a bony, keratin-covered projection forming their mouth. This bill is frequently evolved for specific bird diet types, and many birds also use their bills as tools for carrying, drilling, preening and other tasks.

Warm-Blooded: All birds are endothermic, which means they generate their own internal body heat and do not rely exclusively on their environment to maintain their temperature. While many birds will sun themselves to help regulate their temperature, sunning has more than on purpose and is not solely for body temperature maintenance.

High Metabolism: Birds have a high, efficient metabolism that quickly turns food into usable energy. They have a four-chambered heart and high respiratory rate as well, which helps them be efficient and agile fliers as well as maintain their high body temperatures.

Bipedal: All birds have two legs used for perching, walking, hopping or running. Different types of birds have evolved different leg shapes and lengths to suit their needs; for example, wading birds have thin, long legs suitable for moving through deeper water, while raptors have thicker, more powerful legs for capturing prey.

Furcula: Though not visible to birders, every bird has a furcula, or wishbone, that protects the chest cavity during wing beats. This keeps the bird's chest organs safe from excessive pressure.

Egg-Laying: All birds lay amniotic eggs as part of their reproductive cycle. The eggs have a hard shell and require incubation to continue development until hatching. Egg size, shape and markings varies for each bird species, as does the number of eggs laid, necessary incubation time and the condition of the chicks at hatching.

Communication: Birds have highly developed communication skills, and many bird species communicate vocally through elaborate songs and calls. Nonverbal bird sounds are also part of their communication abilities, and for many species, extensive communication is part of courtship behaviour, territorial defense, parent-chick recognition and community cooperation.

Navigation: Migratory and non-migratory birds alike have keen navigational skills. For migrating species, those skills allow them to make journeys of hundreds or thousands of miles through highly variable climate and geographical conditions, yet arrive at the same places year after year. Non-migratory birds also use their navigation skills to visit the same food sources or nesting sites without difficulty.

All Birds Are the Same, But Different

Many other animals share some characteristics with birds, but only birds represent all the features above to belong to the Class Aves. At the same time, all birds are different, and through the 150 million years of evolution since the Mesozoic Era when birds first evolved from reptiles, small differences have created the roughly 10,000 bird species we enjoy today. Yet with every one of those species, all of these common characteristics are present, making each one a related but distinct bird.

- The Ostrich is the largest bird in the world. It also lays the largest eggs and has the fastest maximum running speed (97 kph).
- Scientists believe that birds evolved from theropod dinosaurs.
- Birds have hollow bones which help them fly.
- Some bird species are intelligent enough to create and use tools.
- The chicken is the most common species of bird found in the world.
- Kiwis are endangered, flightless birds that live in New Zealand. They lay the largest eggs relative to their body size of any bird in the world.

- Hummingbirds can fly backwards.
- The Bee Hummingbird is the smallest living bird in the world, with a length of just 5 cm (2 in).
- Around 20 per cent of bird species migrate long distances every year.
- Homing pigeons are bred to find their way home from long distances away and have been used for thousands of years to carry messages.

Birds make up a special group of vertebrates called aves. Birds and reptiles have many shared traits. Both lay eggs, have similar eyes and brain, similar skull and ear bones, partially hollow bones and similar blood proteins. Birds have some very different traits from their relatives, such as feathers instead of scales, pointed beaks, and wings. All birds are warm-blooded. People who study birds are called ornithologists.

Birds are one of the six basic groups of animals.

- Birds, best known for their ability to fly, are unmatched in their command of the skies.
- Albatrosses glide long distances over the open sea, hummingbirds hover motionless in mid-air, and eagles swoop down to capture prey with pinpoint accuracy.
- But not all birds are aerobatic experts. Some species such as kiwis and penguins, lost their ability to fly long ago in favour of lifestyles suited more for land or water.

Birds are divided into 30 groups

There are 9,865 species of birds alive today. Of the 9,865 bird species:

- 1,227 species are considered threatened with extinction
- 838 species are near threatened
- 7,735 species are considered to be of least concern
- 65 species lack the data to determine their status
- 133 species of birds are known to have gone extinct since 1500.

There are also four species of birds that are classified as extinct in the wild. The last living members of those species survive only in captivity.

- The earliest known bird, Archaeopteryx lithographica, lived about 150 million years ago during the Jurassic Period. Archaeopteryx possessed a blend of reptilian and avian characteristics. It had feathers and wings but instead of a bill it had a reptilian snout.  Archaeopteryx did not have a keeled breastbone, a key feature for flight, so scientists are uncertain whether it was capable of true flight or if it merely glided. A total of ten Archaeopteryx fossil specimens have been unearthed over the years. All of these fossils were recovered from the limestone deposits in quarries near Solnhofen, Germany. The first Archaeopteryx skeleton, now known as the 'London Specimen', was discovered in 1861.
- Evolutionary biologists remain uncertain as to the origin of birds. The fossil record for early birds lacks sufficient detail for evolutionary biologists to determine with much certainty which group of reptiles gave rise to birds. Research currently supports the view that birds evolved from a group of dinosaurs known as theropods during the Mesozoic Era. Modern birds share many characteristics with theropods. Both have hollow bones, a pelvis bone that points backward, a wishbone, and a three-toed foot.
- Feathers are unique to birds. Feathers are a defining characteristic of the group, meaning simply that if an animal has feathers, then it is a bird. Feathers serve many functions in birds but most notable is the critical role feathers play in enabling birds to fly. In addition to helping to enable flight, feathers also provide protection from the elements. Feathers provide birds with waterproofing and insulation and even block harmful UV rays from reaching birds' skin.

- Birds are not the only animals that are capable of flight. Flight is not a characteristic restricted to birds. Bats, which are mammals, fly with great agility and insects, which are arthropods, were fluttering through the air several million years before birds took to the wing.
- All birds reproduce by laying eggs. Eggs vary in size and colour depending on species. Although there is a wide range of egg colours, only two pigments contribute to the colour of the shell. The first pigment is derived from hemoglobin and the second from bile. Most species lay their eggs in a nest. Nests may vary in size, shape, and construction material, but the most common nest shape is cup-shaped.
- Many birds undertake seasonal migrations between their breeding and wintering grounds. Many species of birds migrate to high latitudes to breed during the spring and summer. Then during the fall and winter months they migrate to regions of lower latitude. Many species follow similar routes each year when migrating. These routes are referred to as migratory flyways.
- Birds do not have teeth. Instead they have bills that are made of the protein keratin. Bird bills come in a variety of shapes and sizes and are adapted to the particular diet of each species. Herons, for example, have a sharp, pointed bill that enable them to capture fish. Finches on the other hand have a short, conical bill that is well-suited for cracking open seeds.
- The largest of all birds is the ostrich. Ostriches are flightless birds that have a large body, small head, long legs, and a long neck. Although they cannot fly, they are remarkable runners, able to run at speeds of up to 45 mph for half an hour. Adult ostriches weigh between 220 and 350 pounds and measure between 7 and 9 1/4 feet in height.

More Bird Facts

- The chicken is the closest living relative to the Tyrannosaurus Rex.
- Many birds kept as pets, including doves, parakeets, and lovebirds, enjoy living in pairs for companionship.
- The smallest bird egg belongs to the hummingbird and is the size of a pea. The largest bird egg, from which the ostrich hatches, is the size of a cantaloupe.
- A bird's eye takes up about 50 percent of its head; our eyes take up about 5 percent of our head. To be comparable to a bird's eyes, our eyes would have to be the size of baseballs.
- The penguin is the only bird that can swim, but not fly. It is also the only bird that walks upright.
- Owls turn their heads almost 360° (a complete circle) but they cannot move their eyes.
- Chickens have over 200 distinct noises they make for communicating.
- When it comes to birds, the males tend to have the more glamorous feather shape, coloration, songs, and dances. Female birds choose their mate based on how attractive they find them!
- It is estimated that one third of all bird owners turn on a radio or their pet when they leave the house.
- According to National Geographic, scientists have an answer for the age old dispute over which came first, the chicken or the egg. Reptiles were laying eggs thousands of years before chickens appeared. The first chicken came from an egg laid by a bird that was not quite a chicken. Therefore, the egg came first.
- The first bird domesticated by humans was the goose.
- Kiwi birds are blind, so they hunt by smell.
- Some breeds of chickens can lay coloured eggs. The Ameraucana and Araucana can lay green or blue eggs.

- The common phrase 'eat like a bird' should mean something quite different! Many birds eat twice their weight in food each day. In fact, a bird requires more food in proportion to its size than a baby or a cat.
- A group of larks is called an exaltation, a group of chickens is called a peep, a group of geese is called a gaggle, a group of ravens is called a murder, and a group of owls is called a parliament.
- Chickens that lay brown eggs have red ear lobes. There is a genetic link between the two.
- Crows have the largest cerebral hemispheres (brains), relative to body size, of any avian family.
- Mockingbirds can imitate many sounds, from a squeaking door to a cat meowing.

5 Insect World

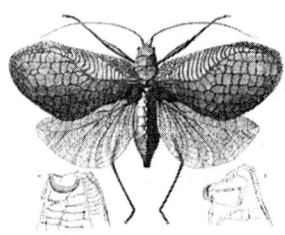

Insects are a class of invertebrates within the arthropod phylum that have a chitinous exoskeleton, a three-part body, three pairs of jointed legs, compound eyes and one pair of antennae.

- The number of insect species is believed to be between six and ten million.
- Insect bodies have three parts, the thorax, abdomen and head.
- Insects have two antennae.
- Insects have three pairs of legs.
- Some insects, such as gerridae (water striders), are able to walk on the surface of water.
- Bees, termites and ants live in well organized social colonies.
- Only male crickets chirp.
- Insects are cold blooded.
- Silkworms are used as the primary producer of silk.
- Most insects hatch from eggs.
- Some cicadas can make sounds nearly 120 decibels loud.

- The life cycle of a mosquito features four stages, egg, larva, pupa and adult.
- Female mosquitoes drink blood in order to obtain nutrients needed to produce eggs.
- Spiders are not insects.
- Bees are found on every continent except Antarctica.
- Ants leave trails and communicate with each other using pheromones as chemical signals.

Amazing Facts About Insects and Bugs

- Night butterflies have ears on their wings so they can avoid bats.
- Monarch caterpillars shed their skin four times before they become a chrysalis, growing over 2700 times their original size.
- There may be as many as 3,000 different kinds of insects—more than all the other animal and plant species combined.
- Of the huge numbers of insects, only a tiny amount, one percent, are harmful to humans. Most insects are harmless or actually beneficial. For example, without bees to pollinate flowers, plants would not have a way of reproducing and we wouldn't have anything to eat!
- Locusts can eat their own weight in food in a day. A person eats his own body weight in about half a year.
- The earliest fossil cockroach is about 280 million years old, 80 million years older than the first dinosaurs!
- The desert locust is the world's most destructive insect. It can eat it's own weight in food every day. Large swarms can gobble up to 20,000 tons of grain and plants in a day.
- The honeybee has to travel an average of 43,000 miles to collect enough nectar to make a pound of honey!
- Out of every 1,000 Mosquitos, one female carries a disease that could be fatal to humans.
- Honeybees have hair on their eyes.
- The average housefly lives for one month.
- There is only one insect that can turn its head—the praying mantis.

- A slug has four noses.
- Some male spiders pluck their cobwebs like a guitar, to attract female spiders.
- A mosquito flaps its wings 500 times a second.
- Only male crickets can chirp.
- Baby robins eat 14 feet of earthworms every day!
- About 80 per cent of the Earth's animals are insects!

- The common garden worm has five pairs of hearts.
- Dragonflies can fly up to 50 miles per hour.
- One kind of insect called a spittlebug, lays its eggs in a big nest of saliva bubbles. I guess no predator would look for a meal in there!
- The heaviest insect in the world weights 2.5 ounces.
- A cockroach can live for up to 3 weeks without its head!
- A butterfly has its taste receptors in its feet!
- The mayfly only lives for 8 hours!
- The female black widow's poison is 15 times deadlier than a rattlesnake's!
- There are worms in Australia that are over 4 feet long!
- The weight of all the termites in the world outweigh the weight of all humans 10 to 1!

More Insect Facts

- Slugs have 4 noses.
- The leech has 32 brains.
- Butterflies taste with their hind feet.
- A snail can sleep for three years.
- Bees have five eyes. There are 3 small eyes on the top of a bee's head and 2 larger ones in front.
- A dragonfly has a lifespan of 24 hours.
- A bee must visit 4000 flowers in order to make one tablespoon of honey.
- A bee can see the colors green, blue and ultra-violet, but red

looks like black.
- The silkworm moth has eleven brains.
- A dragonfly can spot an insect moving 33 feet away.
- Australian termites have been known to build mounds twenty feet high and at least 100 feet wide.
- The average garden variety caterpillar has 248 muscles in its head.
- Ants don't sleep.
- The largest cockroach on record is one measured at 3.81 inches in length.
- Dragonflies are one of the fastest insects, flying 100kmh.
- The blood of insects is yellow.
- Honeybees may collect pollen from as many as 500 flowers, all of the same species, in a single trip.
- Ticks can be as small as a grain of rice and grow to be as big as a marble.
- Flies have 4000 lenses in each eye.
- Houseflies watch each other constantly and follow each other to food sources. That's why there are always so many enjoying the same food.
- Spiders have noses on their feet that can pick up the odours of possible prey, predators, or mates.
- Adult fleas can live for up to 2 years during which time the female can lay up to 1200 eggs.
- Dragonflies have the largest eyes and sharpest eyesight of any insect. Each eye is made up of more than 30,000 separate rod-like units.
- Centipedes always have an uneven pairs of walking legs.
- A butterfly has to have a body temperature greater than 86 degrees to be able to fly.
- Mosquitoes have 47 teeth.
- A snail's reproductive organs are in its head.
- Only full-grown male crickets can chirp.
- The praying mantis only has one ear.
- Insects are the only invertebrates with wings.
- A botfly is known to fly at a speed of 1300 km/hr, which makes

it faster then an aircraft.
- The brain of a cockroach is located within its body, so even if it were to lose its head, the roach can survive for 9 days before it would finally die of hunger.
- An earthworm has the capacity to pull a weight, which exceed 10 times its own body weight.
- Fleas are known to cover a distance of 30 cm in a single leap, i.e. twenty times the length of their own body.
- Tarantulas can survive without food for more than two years.
- An ant uses its antenna for touch as well as smell.
- An ant has two stomachs, in one stomach it stores food for itself and in the other it stores food that is to be shared with other ants.
- Queen ants are provided with wings at birth, they lose these wings after they fly off to start new colonies.
- A Tropical Leafcutter ant uses its sharp outer jaw to cut leaves and make them into pulp. The pulp is later used to make fungus gardens. These gardens are looked after and harvested for food.
- Worker ants are given the responsibility of taking the rubbish from the nest and putting it into the rubbish dump.
- When a worker ant finds a source of food, it leaves a trail of scent to attract other ants in the colony to it.

6 Mountain World

- Mountains make up about one-fifth of the world's landscape, and provide homes to at least one-tenth of the world's people.
- Heights of mountains are generally given as heights above sea level.
- The world's highest peak on land is Mount Everest in the Himalayas. It is 8,850.1728 m (29,036 ft) tall.
- Ben Nevis is also the highest mountain in Great Britain.
- The tallest known mountain in the solar system is Olympus Mons, located on Mars.
- There are mountains under the surface of the sea!
- Mountains occur more often in oceans than on land; some islands are the peaks of mountains coming out of the water.

- About 80 per cent of our planet's fresh water originates in the mountains.
- All mountain ecosystems have one major characteristic in common—rapid changes in altitude, climate, soil, and vegetation over very short distances.
- Plants that may be found on mountains include conifers, oak, chestnut, maple, junipers, stonecrops, campions, mosses, ferns and climbers.
- The highest 14 mountains in the world are all found in the Himalayas.
- In some mountainous areas the rivers are permanently frozen. These are called glaciers.

World Mountains

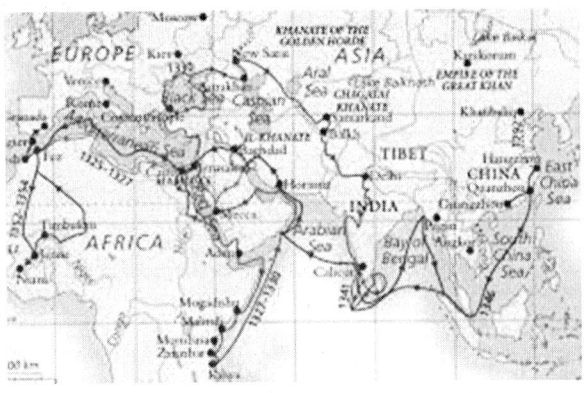

Asia

Asia is the largest continent in both size and population covering almost 1/3 of the world's land area and it has about 3/5 of the world's people. It has some of the world's highest mountains, longest rivers, largest deserts, plains and plateaus, and thickest forests and jungles.

- Nepal: Mount Everest, is the highest mountain on the earth (measuring from sea level). It rises 8,848 metres above the sea, on the border between Nepal and China.
- K2 is the second highest mountain on the earth. It rises 8,611ms above sea level.

> **INSIDE OUT**
> Everest has three names. In the Nepali language it is called Sagarmatha (Head of the Sky), and in Tibetan it is called Chomolangma (short for Jomo Miyolangsangma, the name of a Tibetan goddess who is one of the Five Sisters of Long Life).

Japan:

Mount Fuji, (highest mountain in Japan) 3,776ms: It is an isolated volcano, located only 50 miles southwest from Tokyo.

Britain:

- Ben Nevis—highest mountain in Great Britain—Ben Nevis, Scotland 1,343ms
- Snowdon—highest mountain in Wales
- Scafell Pike—highest mountain in England (978 metres = 3208 feet high)
- Kinder Scout—highest peak in the Peak District

Greece:

Mount Olympus is the highest mountain in Greece. Mount Olympus, Athens 2,917ms

Turkey:

Mount Ararat is a snow-capped volcanic cone, located in extreme northeast Turkey. Mount Ararat, 5,165ms

Africa:

Africa is the second largest continent in area covering about 1/5 of the world's land area and it has the third largest population. Volcanic activity created most of Africa's highest mountains.

The 2 tallest peaks are Mt. Kilimanjaro at 19,340 ft. and Mt. Kenya at 17,058 ft. They are both extinct volcanoes. Even though both mountains rise near to the equator, they have glaciers and are covered with snow most of the year.

Tanzania:

The highest mountain in Africa, located in northeast Tanzania, near the Kenya border. Mount Kilimanjaro, 5,895ms

Kenya:

The second highest mountain in Africa. Like Mount Kilimanjaro, it is an extinct volcano. Mount Kenya, 5,199ms

Australia:

- The highest mountain in Australia, located in the extreme southeast corner of the continent. Located between Melbourne and Sydney in the Australian Alps, Mt Kosciuszko, Australia, 2228 metres
- Ayers Rock, Northern Australia, 335ms
- Mount Bruce, Australia, 1227ms

South America:

Aconcagua is the highest mountain in the Western hemisphere, located in western Argentina, near the Chile border. Argentina: Aconcagua in Andes 6,960ms

7 Cities of the World

The largest cities in the world by land area, population and density Ranked by population: 1 to 125. The top four:

Rank	City/Urban area	Country
1	Tokyo/Yokohama	Japan
2	New York Metro	USA
3	Sao Paulo	Brazil
4	Seoul/Incheon	South Korea

Largest cities in the world ranked by population (1 to 125)

Rank	City / Urban area	Country	Population	Land area (in sqKm)	Density (people per sqKm)
1	Tokyo/Yokohama	Japan	33,200,000	6,993	4,750
2	New York Metro	USA	17,800,000	8,683	2,050
3	Sao Paulo	Brazil	17,700,000	1,968	9,000
4	Seoul/Incheon	South Korea	17,500,000	1,049	16,700
5	Mexico City	Mexico	17,400,000	2,072	8,400
6	Osaka/Kobe/Kyoto	Japan	16,425,000	2,564	6,400
7	Manila	Philippines	14,750,000	1,399	10,550
8	Mumbai	India	14,350,000	484	29,650
9	Delhi	India	14,300,000	1,295	11,050
10	Jakarta	Indonesia	14,250,000	1,360	10,500
11	Lagos	Nigeria	13,400,000	738	18,150
12	Kolkata	India	12,700,000	531	23,900
13	Cairo	Egypt	12,200,000	1,295	9,400
14	Los Angeles	USA	11,789,000	4,320	2,750
15	Buenos Aires	Argentina	11,200,000	2,266	4,950
16	Rio de Janeiro	Brazil	10,800,000	1,580	6,850
17	Moscow	Russia	10,500,000	2,150	4,900
18	Shanghai	China	10,000,000	746	13,400
19	Karachi	Pakistan	9,800,000	518	18,900
20	Paris	France	9,645,000	2,723	3,550
21	Istanbul	Turkey	9,000,000	1,166	7,700
22	Nagoya	Japan	9,000,000	2,875	3,150
23	Beijing	China	8,614,000	748	11,500
24	Chicago	USA	8,308,000	5,498	1,500
25	London	UK	8,278,000	1,623	5,100

26	Shenzhen	China	8,000,000	466	17,150
27	Essen/Düsseldorf	Germany	7,350,000	2,642	2,800
28	Tehran	Iran	7,250,000	686	10,550
29	Bogota	Colombia	7,000,000	518	13,500
30	Lima	Peru	7,000,000	596	11,750
31	Bangkok	Thailand	6,500,000	1,010	6,450
32	Johannesburg/East Rand	South Africa	6,000,000	2,396	2,500
33	Chennai	India	5,950,000	414	14,350
34	Taipei	Taiwan	5,700,000	376	15,200
35	Baghdad	Iraq	5,500,000	596	9,250
36	Santiago	Chile	5,425,000	648	8,400
37	Bangalore	India	5,400,000	534	10,100
38	Hyderabad	India	5,300,000	583	9,100
39	St Petersburg	Russia	5,300,000	622	8,550
40	Philadelphia	USA	5,149,000	4,661	1,100
41	Lahore	Pakistan	5,100,000	622	8,200
42	Kinshasa	Congo	5,000,000	469	10,650
43	Miami	USA	4,919,000	2,891	1,700
44	Ho Chi Minh City	Vietnam	4,900,000	518	9,450
45	Madrid	Spain	4,900,000	945	5,200
46	Tianjin	China	4,750,000	453	10,500
47	Kuala Lumpur	Malaysia	4,400,000	1,606	2,750
48	Toronto	Canada	4,367,000	1,655	2,650
49	Milan	Italy	4,250,000	1,554	2,750
50	Shenyang	China	4,200,000	453	9,250
51	Dallas/Fort Worth	USA	4,146,000	3,644	1,150
52	Boston	USA	4,032,000	4,497	900
53	Belo Horizonte	Brazil	4,000,000	868	4,600
54	Khartoum	Sudan	4,000,000	583	6,850

55	Riyadh	Saudi Arabia	4,000,000	1,101	3,650
56	Singapore	Singapore	4,000,000	479	8,350
57	Washington	USA	3,934,000	2,996	1,300
58	Detroit	USA	3,903,000	3,267	1,200
59	Barcelona	Spain	3,900,000	803	4,850
60	Houston	USA	3,823,000	3,355	1,150
61	Athens	Greece	3,685,000	684	5,400
62	Berlin	Germany	3,675,000	984	3,750
63	Sydney	Australia	3,502,000	1,687	2,100
64	Atlanta	USA	3,500,000	5,083	700
65	Guadalajara	Mexico	3,500,000	596	5,900
66	San Francisco/Oakland	USA	3,229,000	1,365	2,350
67	Montreal	Canada	3,216,000	1,740	1,850
68	Monterey	Mexico	3,200,000	479	6,700
69	Melbourne	Australia	3,162,000	2,080	1,500
70	Ankara	Turkey	3,100,000	583	5,300
71	Recife	Brazil	3,025,000	376	8,050
72	Phoenix/Mesa	USA	2,907,000	2,069	1,400
73	Durban	South Africa	2,900,000	829	3,500
74	Porto Alegre	Brazil	2,800,000	583	4,800
75	Dalian	China	2,750,000	389	7,100
76	Jeddah	Saudi Arabia	2,750,000	777	3,550
77	Seattle	USA	2,712,000	2,470	1,100
78	Cape Town	South Africa	2,700,000	686	3,950
79	San Diego	USA	2,674,000	2,026	1,300
80	Fortaleza	Brazil	2,650,000	583	4,550
81	Curitiba	Brazil	2,500,000	648	3,850
82	Rome	Italy	2,500,000	842	2,950

83	Naples	Italy	2,400,000	583	4,100
84	Minneapolis/St. Paul	USA	2,389,000	2,316	1,050
85	Tel Aviv	Israel	2,300,000	453	5,050
86	Birmingham	UK	2,284,000	600	3,800
87	Frankfurt	Germany	2,260,000	984	2,300
88	Lisbon	Portugal	2,250,000	881	2,550
89	Manchester	UK	2,245,000	558	4,000
90	San Juan	Puerto Rico	2,217,000	2,309	950
91	Katowice	Poland	2,200,000	544	4,050
92	Tashkent	Uzbekistan	2,200,000	531	4,150
93	Fukuoka	Japan	2,150,000	544	3,950
94	Baku/Sumqayit	Azerbaijan	2,100,000	544	3,850
95	St. Louis	USA	2,078,000	2,147	950
96	Baltimore	USA	2,076,000	1,768	1,150
97	Sapporo	Japan	2,075,000	414	5,000
98	Tampa/St. Petersburg	USA	2,062,000	2,078	1,000
99	Taichung	Taiwan	2,000,000	510	3,900
100	Warsaw	Poland	2,000,000	466	4,300
101	Denver	USA	1,985,000	1,292	1,550
102	Cologne/Bonn	Germany	1,960,000	816	2,400
103	Hamburg	Germany	1,925,000	829	2,300
104	Dubai	UAE	1,900,000	712	2,650
105	Pretoria	South Africa	1,850,000	673	2,750
106	Vancouver	Canada	1,830,000	1,120	1,650
107	Beirut	Lebanon	1,800,000	648	2,800
108	Budapest	Hungary	1,800,000	702	2,550
109	Cleveland	USA	1,787,000	1,676	1,050

110	Pittsburgh	USA	1,753,000	2,208	800
111	Campinas	Brazil	1,750,000	492	3,550
112	Harare	Zimbabwe	1,750,000	712	2,450
113	Brasilia	Brazil	1,625,000	583	2,800
114	Kuwait	Kuwait	1,600,000	544	2,950
115	Munich	Germany	1,600,000	518	3,100
116	Portland	USA	1,583,000	1,228	1,300
117	Brussels	Belgium	1,570,000	712	2,200
118	Vienna	Austria	1,550,000	453	3,400
119	San Jose	USA	1,538,000	674	2,300
120	Dammam	Saudi Arabia	1,525,000	673	2,250
121	Copenhagen	Denmark	1,525,000	816	1,850
122	Brisbane	Australia	1,508,000	1,603	950
123	Riverside/San Bernardino	USA	1,507,000	1,136	1,350
124	Cincinnati	USA	1,503,000	1,740	850
125	Accra	Ghana	1,500,000	453	3,300

The Major Cities of the World

Japan

Tokyo

Tokyo is the capital of Japan located on the eastern coast of Honshu Island at the head of Tokyo Bay. The city of Tokyo is the administrative, financial, educational, cultural and industrial center of Japan, surrounded by numerous suburban manufacturing complexes.

Seoul
The Republic of Korea

Seoul is the capital of the Republic of Korea (South Korea), located in northwest part of the country, on the Han River. The political, commercial, industrial, and cultural center of the nation, Seoul is by far the most important city in the country.

Pyongyang
Democratic People's Republic of Korea

Pyongyang is the capital of North Korea, in southwest of the country, on a high bluff looking down the Taedong River. It is considered as the oldest city on the Korean Peninsula. During the Korean War, Pyongyang fell to the North Koreans. After having been ravaged in the war, the city was rebuilt according to an organised city planning.

Evening Skyline
Pyongyang, D.P.R. Korea

Ulan Bator
Mongolia

Ulan Bator (Ulaan Baatar) is the capital city of Mongolia, situated in the north central part of the country, on the Tuul River. It is situated at the foot of the Bogdo Khan Uul. It is the political, cultural, economic, and transportation center of the country.

Beijing
People's Republic of China

Beijing is the capital of the People's Republic of China. The second largest city in China (after Shanghai), Beijing is the political, cultural, and educational center of the country. At the center of the city, Tianmen square is located surrounded by Great Hall of the People to the west and Museum of the Revolution to the east.

Taipei
Taiwan

Taipei is the capital of Taiwan located in the northern part of Taiwan Island. Taiwan's largest city, it is the administrative, cultural, and industrial center of the island. The Jiang Jie–shi Memorial Park is located in the centre of the city.

Manila
Republic of the Philippines

Manila is the capital of Republic of the Philippines, southwest Luzon, on Manila Bay. Manila is the center of the country's largest metropolitan area, with its chief port, and the center of all the governmental, commercial, industrial, and cultural activities.

Hanoi
Socialist Republic of Vietnam

Hanoi is the capital of Vietnam, on the right bank of the Red River. Hanoi became (7th century) the seat of the

Chinese rulers of Vietnam. Hanoi was occupied briefly by French in 1873 and it became the capital of French Indochina after 1887.

Vientian
Lao People's Democratic Republic

Vientiane is the administrative capital and the largest city of Laos, in the north central part of the country on the Mekong River. Vientiane possesses diverse light industries and is a trading centre of forest products, textiles, and hides.

Xieng Khuan

Phnom Penh
Kingdom of Cambodia

Phnom Penh is the capital of Cambodia, in southwest part of the contry, at the confluence of the Mekong and Tonle Sap rivers. Phnom Penh was founded in the 14th century and became Khmer capital after the abandonment of Angkor. It became the capital of Cambodia in 1867. The cultural and commercial centre as well as political capital of Cambodia.

Bangkok
Kingdom of Thailand

Bangkok is the capital of Thailand, in southwest part of the country, on the east bank of the Chao Phraya River, near the Gulf of Thailand. Thailand's largest city and one of the leading cities of southeast Asia. Bangkok is home to the regional headquarters of the UN Economic and Social Commission for Asia and the Pacific (ESCAP), as well as many other international businesses and organisations.

Kuala Lumpur
Malaysia

Kuala Lumpur is the capital of Malaysia, located in the southern part of Malay Peninsula, at the confluence of the Klang and Gombak rivers. Malaysia's chief inland city, Kuala Lumpur is the country's commercial and transportation hub.

Singapore
Republic of Singapore

Singapore, officially called Republic of Singapore, consists of the mainland of Singapore and about 50 small adjacent islands at the southern tip of the Malay Peninsula, southeast Asia. Its Capital, Singapore city is the largest city and historically played an important role as a key junction of trade between Pacific Ocean and Indian Ocean.

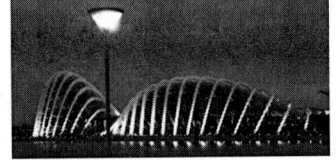

Jakarta
Republic of Indonesia

Jakarta is the capital and largest city of Indonesia located in northwest Java island, at the mouth of the canalized Ciliwung River, on Jakarta Bay. It is the country's administrative, commercial, industrial, and transportation center.

Yangon
Union of Myanmar

Yangon, formerly Rangoon, is the capital of Myanmar and of Yangon div., located in the south central of Myanmar, on the Yangon River. The name of Yangon, meaning 'the end of war' was given in 1755, ever since the city has been developed as a port city, the center of commercial activities. Central part of the city was constructed according to the city planning in 1952, when beautiful grid street scape was developed.

Dhaka
People's Republic of Bangladesh

Dhaka is the capital of Bangladesh, located in the high populated delta prone to floods on a channel of the Dhaleswari River, in the heart of the world's largest jute-growing region, and the industrial, commercial, and administrative centre of Bangladesh. The city achieved glory as the 17th-century Mughal capital of Bengal and became the capital of Pakistan in 1971.

Katmandu
Kingdom of Nepal

Katmandu is the capital of Nepal, central Nepal in a fertile valley of the Himalayas. It is the administrative, business, and commercial centre of Nepal. Great many western tourists visit Katmandu, many of them mountain climbers. Tourism and trade with India led to a rapid increase in Katmandu's population and to the expansion of paved streets and sewage systems.

New Delhi
India

Delhi is located in the middle of Delhi plain, where Yamuna River crosses. New Delhi, the capital of India, and Delhi (or Old Delhi) are the chief urban centers. Government buildings are concentrated in New Delhi, which has organised streets with greens and parks.

Islamabad
Islamic Republic of Pakistan

Islamabad is the capital of Pakistan, in NE part of the country, just NE of Rawalpindi, the former interim capital. Construction of Islamabad (city of Islam) as the capital to replace Karachi began in 1960.

Kabul
Islamic State of Afghanistan

Kabul is the capital of Afghanistan and its largest city and economic and cultural centre, in the east part of the country, on the Kabul River. It is strategically located in a high

narrow valley, between mountain ranges that commands the main approaches to the Khyber Pass. A tunnel under the Hindu Kush mountains links Kabul to the Tajikistan border.

Tashkent
Republic of Uzbekistan

Tashkent is the capital of Tashkent region and of Uzbekistan, in the foothills of the Tian Shan mountains. The largest and one of the oldest cities of Central Asia, it is the economic heart of the region.

Tehran
Islamic Republic of Iran

Tehran is the capital of Iran, in north part of the country, near Mt. Damavand. It is Iran's largest city and its administrative, commercial, and industrial centre. Meherabad international airport is located in the centre of the image, and Azadi Tower (Freedom Tower), which was built for the celebrations of the 2500th anniversary of the monarchy, is located at the junction of the roads from the airport, and acts as a gateway to the capital.

Baghdad
Republic of Iraq

Baghdad is the capital of Iraq, located in the central Iraq, on both banks of the Tigris River. The city was founded (762) on the west bank of the Tigris by the Abbasid caliph Mansur, who made it his capital. The period of its utmost glory is reflected in the Thousand and One Nights, in which many of the tales are set in Baghdad. Now, the city's principal economic activity is oil industry, as a result, Baghdad experienced rapid economic and population growth.

Riyadh
Kingdom of Saudi Arabia

Riyadh is the capital and the largest city of Saudi Arabia, located in the Nejd district, central part of Saudi Arabia. Situated in an oasis, Riyadh is the nation's educational, administrative, financial, and transportation center. Oil refining is the main industry.

Jerusalem
State of Israel
Jerusalem is the capital of Israel. It is situated on a ridge of 760 m high that lies west of the Dead Sea and the Jordan River. Jerusalem is the center of administrative, religious, educational, cultural, and market activities. Tourism and construction are the city's major industries.

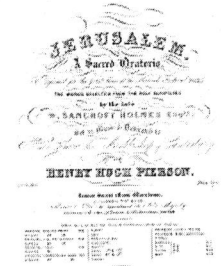

Cairo
Arab Republic of Egypt
Cairo is the capital of Egypt in northeast part of the country. The city includes two islands in the Nile, Zamalik (Gezira) and Roda (Rawdah), which are linked to the mainland by bridges. Cairo is the largest city in the Middle East and in Africa. It is Egypt's administrative center and, along with Alexandria, the heart of its economic activities.

Tunis
Republic of Tunisia
Tunis is the capital of Tunisia, in northeast part of the county, on the Lake of Tunis. Access to the Gulf of Tunis (an arm of the Mediterranean) is by a canal terminating at a subsidiary port, Halq al Wadi (La Goulette). Tunis has notable mosques, the Univ. of Tunis, and a national museum. The ruins of Carthage are located nearby, to the northeast in the right of the image.

Casablanca
Kingdom of Morocco

Casablanca is the largest city and principal port of Morocco, located in the western part of Morocco, on the Atlantic Ocean. It accounts for more than half of Morocco's industrial production. During World War II, Casablanca was the scene of one of the three major Allied landings in North Africa (Nov., 1942) and the conference between Franklin Delano Roosevelt and Winston Churchill was held (Nov., 1943).

Johannesburg
Republic of South Africa

Johannesburg is the largest city in South Africa, the centre of its important gold–mining industry, its manufacturing and commercial center, and the hub of its transportation network. Gold mining is the sprawling city's chief industry. Manufactures include cut diamonds, industrial chemicals, plastics, cement, electrical, electronic, and mining equipment, paper and paper products, glass, food products and beer.

Istanbul
Republic of Turkey

Istanbul is the largest city in Turkey on both sides of the Bosporus at its entrance into the Sea of Marmara. Its name was officially changed from Constantinople to Istanbul in 1930; before A.D. 330 it was known as Byzantium. In cities adjacent to Europe, Overseas Establishments, hotels, restaurants and shops are concentrated, while old cities adjacent to Asia has landmark constructions represented by Blue Mosque, Ayasofya, Topkapi Sarayi and Kapali Carsi, commemorating Greek, Rome and Ottman Enpire.

Athens

Hellenic Republic

Athens is the capital of Greece, eastern central Greece, on the plain of Attica, between the Kifisos and Ilissus rivers, near the Saronic Gulf. Mt. Aigaleos, Mt. Parnis, Mt. Pendelikon, and Mt. Hymettus are lined in a semicircle with the city at its  centre. The capital of Attica prefecture, Athens is the largest city in Greece and it is administrative, economic, and cultural centre. In the city there are many landmarks, major one is the acropolis which dominates the city and on which stand the remains of the Parthenon.

Kiev

Ukraine

Kiev is the capital of Ukraine with a port on the Dnieper River. The largest city of Ukraine, Kiev is the industrial, commercial, and cultural centre. Known to Russians as the mother of cities, Kiev is one of the oldest towns in the north  Europe. Lying amid hills along the Dnieper and filled with gardens and parks, Kiev is one of Europe's most beautiful cities, as well as a treasury of medieval art and architecture.

Moscow
Russian Federation

Moscow is the capital of Russia and the administrative centre of the Central district, in the western central European Russia, on the Moskva River near its junction with the Moscow Canal.

In the city, roads spread in concentric circles with Kremlin at the center, dividing the city into several divisions. The outermost division is allocated as a residental area. A loop road surrounding the area is the boundary of the city.

St. Petersburg
Russian Federation

Sankt Petersburg, the second largest city and former capital in Russia, formerly named Leningrad at the head of the Gulf of Finland on both banks of the Neva River and on the islands of its delta. The city's main thoroughfare is the celebrated Nevsky Prospekt. On it are the high–spired admiralty building; the Winter Palace; the Hermitage museum; the huge domed Cathedral of St. Isaac; and the equestrian statue of Peter the Great.

Rome
Republic of Italy

Rome is the capital of Italy and see of the pope, whose residence, Vatican City, is a sovereign state within the city of Rome. Rome is also the capital of Latium, a region in central part of Italy, and of Rome prov. It lies on both banks of the Tiber and its affluent, the Aniene, in the Campagna di Roma, between the Apennine Mts. and the

Tyrrhenian Sea. Called the Eternal City, it is one of the world's richest cities in history and art as well as one of its cultural, religious, and intellectual centers.

Paris

French Republic

Paris is the capital of France on the Seine River. It is the commercial and industrial focus of France and a cultural and intellectual center in the world. Paris is divided into roughly equal sections by the Seine. On the right (northern) bank are the Bois de Boulogne, Arc de Triomphe, Place de la Concorde, Opera and Louvre. The left bank, with the Sorbonne, the French Academy, is the governmental and the intellectual section.

Berlin

Federal Republic of Germany

Berlin is the capital of Germany, coextensive with Berlin state, northeast Germany, on the Spree and Havel rivers. Formerly divided into East Berlin and West Berlin, the city was reunified along with East and West Germany on Oct. 3, 1990. The large Tiergarten park

in central Berlin contains the reconstructed Reichstag building with its glass dome and the Berlin zoo. Landmark of the city includes Charlottenburg castle, Kaiser Wilhelm Memorial church, Reichstag and Philharmonic Hall.

Wien

Republic of Austria

Wien (Vienna) is the capital and largest city of Austria and administrative seat of Lower Austria, in the northeast part of the country, on the Danube River. The city plays an important role as a major riverfront town in Europe.

The former residence of the Holy Roman emperors and, after 1806, of the emperors of Austria, Wien is one of the great historic cities of the world and a melting pot of the Germanic, Slav, Italian, and Hungarian peoples and cultures.

London

United Kingdom of Great Britain and Northern Ireland

London is the capital of Great Britain, in the southeast part of England, on both sides of the Thames River. Greater London consists of the 'City of London', or 'City' and 32 boroughs. The City is the commercial center; it is also referred to as the 'Square Mile' because of its areal feature. The 13 inner boroughs that surround the City are Westminster, Camden, Islington, Hackney, Tower Hamlets, Greenwich, Lewisham, Southwark, Lambeth, Wandsworth, Hammersmith and Fulham, Kensington and Chelsea.

Madrid
Spain

Madrid is the capital of Spain located in the central part of the country, and the center of its own autonomous region, on the Manzanares River. Its landmarks include the huge royal palace, opera house, the Buen Retiro park  and three superb art museums, the Prado, which houses one of the finest art collections in the world; the Queen Sofia Museum of modern art; and the Thyssen–Bornemisza Museum; housed in the renovated Villahermosa Palace.

Lisbon
Portuguese Republic

Lisbon is the capital of Portugal on the Tejo River where it broadens to enter the Atlantic Ocean. Lisbon is Portugal's largest city and its cultural, administrative, commercial, and industrial hub. Delta at the mouth of Tejo river provided the optimum location as a harbor in Europe for handling large trades, which led to develop into a major cruise port. In 1966, one of the world's longest suspension bridges was completed across the Tejo.

Vancouver
Canada

Vancouver is a city in southwest British Columbia, Canada, on Burrard Inlet of the Strait of Georgia, opposite Vancouver Island and just north of the Wash. border. It is the largest city on Canada's Pacific coast, the center of the third largest metropolitan area in

Canada, and the nation's chief Pacific port, with an excellent year-round harbor. At Point Grey in metropolitan Vancouver is the Univ. of British Columbia in the lower left of image, and Stanley Park, the largest among the city's parks, is in the top of peninsula in the center of the mage.

New York
United States of America
New York city is the largest city in the United States and one of the largest in the world, on New York Bay at the mouth of the Hudson River. It consists five boroughs, Queens, Brooklyn, State Island, Bronx and Manhattan. Except for Bronx, all the other boroughs are located on island. Central park, which spreads in the central part of Long Island, is said to be the first public buildings to have applied landscape architecture in the US history.

Washington D.C.
United States of America
Washington, D.C. is the capital of the United States, coextensive with the District of Columbia, on the Potomac River. The city is the center of a metropolitan area extending into Maryland and Virginia. Washington is the legislative, administrative, and judicial center of the United States but has little industry; its business is mainly involved in the government, and hundreds of thousands of people are employed in the metropolitan area.

San Francisco
United States of America

San Francisco is a city in western California, on the tip of a peninsula between the Pacific Ocean and San Francisco Bay, which are connected by the strait known as the Golden Gate. The city is the heart of the San Francisco Bay region and with along Oakland and San Jose, the city comprises the fourth largest metropolitan area in the United States.

Los Angeles
United States of America

Los Angeles is a city in south California. It has the second largest population in US cities and it is one of the largest cities as the hub of industries, commercials, transportations, finances and international trades. Two mountain ranges, the Santa Monica and Verdugo, cut across the centre of the city. The east end of the Santa Monica Mountains is seen in the upper left of the image.

Mexico City
United Mexican States

Mexico City is the capital and largest city of Mexico located in the center of the country. Mexico City forms the core of the Federal District and is the commercial, industrial, financial, political, and cultural center of the nation. Population has increased rapidly in a city that had already spread out into many residential sections called colonias.

Brasilia
Federative Republic of Brazil
Brasilia is the capital city and federal district of Brazil located in the southwest of Goias state. Inaugurated in 1960, it is situated in the highlands of central Brazil, and its modern public buildings stand out in sparsely settled countryside. The city was laid out (1957) in the shape of an airplane by the Brazilian architect Lucio Costa. Government services, small-scaled industry, food services, and construction are important factors for the country's economy.

Rio de Janeiro
Federative Republic of Brazil
Rio de Janeiro is the capital of Rio de Janeiro state, in southeast Brazil, on Guanabara Bay of the Atlantic Ocean. The second largest city and former capital of Brazil, it is the cultural center of the country as well as financial, commercial, communication, and transportation hub. Rio has one of the world's most beautiful natural harbors. It is surrounded by low mountain ranges, which extend to the waterside, across the city.

Buenos Aires
Argentine Republic
Buenos Aires is the capital of Argentina located in the east central part of Argentina, on the Rio de la Plata. One of the largest cities in Latin America, Buenos Aires is

Argentina's chief port and financial, industrial, commercial, and social center. Area around a port in the right part of the image is the place where the people first settled. Since then, the city has expanded in semicircle form.

Santiago
Republic of Chile

Santiago is the capital of Chile and of Metropolitana de Santiago region, on the Mapocho River. It is the political, commercial, and financial heart of the nation. The city was founded and named Santiago de Nueva Estremadura on Feb. 12, 1541, by Pedro de Valdivia. Laid out according to Valdivia's plan in a gridiron pattern between the hill of Santa Lucia and the Mapocho, a mountain torrent, Santiago has spread over a broad valley plain and it is one of the largest cities in South America.

Canberra
Commonwealth of Australia

Canberra is the capital of Australia, in the Australian Capital Territory, located in southeast Australia. The city was first settled in 1824, and chosen as the capital in 1908. In 1913, Canberra officially became the second capital of the commonwealth (succeeding Melbourne); however, although the Parliament first met there in 1927, the transfer of federal functions was not completed until after World War II and the Parliament House, on Capitol Hill, was not opened until 1988.

8 Languages of the World

Languages Based on Native Speakers

Mandarin

With more than 955 million speakers, Mandarin claims the top spot as the world's most common language—and one that often requires professional translation services.

One of the five major dialects of Chinese, Mandarin is the official language of China and Taiwan, as well as one of the four official dialects of Singapore. Approximately 14.4 percent of the world's population are native speakers of Mandarin.

Spanish

Its prominence in the Americas as well as in Europe makes Spanish one of the most common languages, with 405 million speakers. The Castilian dialect in Spain is held as a national standard, although Andalusian and Catalan are also spoken.

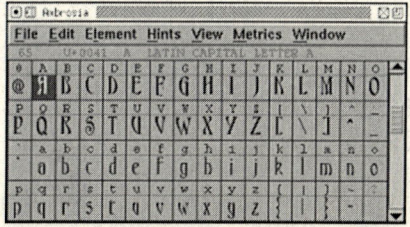

English

English used to be the second-most common language, but Spanish-speakers have increased much more rapidly over the past 15 years. Still, scholars have named English the world's 'most influential language', due to the number of speakers (360 million) and the number of countries in which it is spoken.

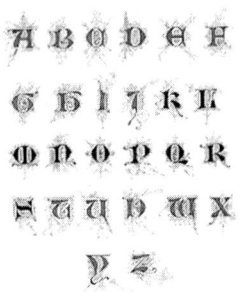

Hindi/Urdu

Although they have different written forms, Hindi and Urdu share a history, many common words, and a grammar. Many linguists consider them different 'registers' of the same common language. Over 310 million people speak one of the two.

Arabic

Arabic, spoken by 295 million speakers worldwide, is also the language of Muslim holy writings. It has also influenced other most common languages—Spanish has approximately 4,000 words with Arabic roots.

Portuguese

Out of the 215 million Portuguese speakers worldwide, nearly 150 million of them speak Brazilian Portuguese, the most common language variant. Portuguese is also the official language of other countries including Angola, Mozambique, and clearly Portugal, among others.

Bengali

With 205 million speakers, Bengali is also the second most widely spoken language in India, popular in the easternmost states. Bengali is an official language of both India and Bangladesh.

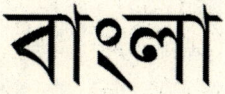

Russian

Russian's 155 million speakers make it the world's eighth most common language. It is also one of the six official languages of the United Nations, along with Arabic, Chinese (Mandarin), English, French and Spanish.

Japanese

Out of the approximately 125 million people who speak Japanese, 124 million live in Japan and the island group of Okinawa. This makes it unusual among the most common languages in its geographic concentration.

Punjabi

Fifteen years ago, German held the tenth spot, though Punjabi has recently surpassed it. With 102 million speakers, Punjabi is mainly spoken in India and Pakistan, and is a native language of 1.44 percent of the world's population.

The 50 Most Widely Spoken Languages

Rank, language	Countries	Population (in millions)
1. Chinese, Mandarin	Brunei, Cambodia, China, Indonesia, Malaysia, Mongolia, Philippines, Singapore, S. Africa, Taiwan, Thailand	1120

Amazing World Facts

2. English	Australia, Belize, Botswana, Brunei, Cameroon, Canada, Eritrea, Ethiopia, Fiji, The Gambia, Ghana, Guyana, India, Ireland, Israel, Lesotho, Liberia, Malaysia, Micronesia, Namibia, Nauru, New Zealand, Palau, Papua New Guinea, Philippines, Samoa, Seychelles, Sierra Leone, Singapore, Solomon Islands, Somalia, S. Africa, Suriname, Swaziland, Tonga, U.K., U.S., Vanuatu, Zimbabwe, many Caribbean states, Zambia.	480
3. Spanish	Algeria, Andorra, Argentina, Belize, Benin, Bolivia, Chad, Chile, Colombia, Costa Rica, Cuba, Dominican Rep., Ecuador, El Salvador, Eq. Guinea, Guatemala, Honduras, Ivory Coast, Madagascar, Mali, Mexico, Morocco, Nicaragua, Niger, Panama, Paraguay, Peru, Spain, Togo, Tunisia, United States, Uruguay, Venezuela.	332
4. Arabic	Egypt, Sudan, ALgeria, Morocco, Tunisia, Lybia, Saudi Arabia, Syria, Jordan, Yemen, UAE, Oman, Iraq, Lebanon	235
5. Bengali	Bangladesh, India, Singapore	189
6. Hindi	India, Nepal, Singapore, South Africa, Uganda	182
7. Russian	Belarus, China, Estonia, Georgia, Israel, Kazakhstan, Kyrgyzstan, Latvia, Lithuania, Moldova, Mongolia, Russia, Turkmenistan, Ukraine, US, Uzbekistan	180

8. Portuguese	Angola, Brazil, Cape Verde, France, Guinea–Bissau, Mozambique, Portugal, São Tomé and Príncipe, Macau	170
9. Japanese	Japan, Singapore, Taiwan	125
10. German	Austria, Belgium, Bolivia, Czech Rep., Denmark, Germany, Hungary, Italy, Kazakhstan, Liechtenstein, Luxembourg, Paraguay, Poland, Romania, Slovakia, Switzerland	98
11. Chinese, Wu	China	77.2
12. Javanese	Indonesia, Malaysia, Singapore	75.5
13. Korean	China, Japan, N. Korea, S. Korea, Singapore, Thailand	75
14. French	Algeria, Andorra, Belgium, Benin, Burkina Faso, Burundi, Cambodia, Cameroon, Canada, Chad, Comoros, Congo, Democratic Republic of the Congo, Djibouti, France, Gabon, Guinea, Haiti, Ivory Coast, Laos, Luxembourg, Madagascar, Mali, Mauritania, Monaco, Morocco, Niger, Rwanda, Senegal, Seychelles, Switzerland, Togo, Tunisia, Vanuatu, Vietnam	72
15. Turkish	Bulgaria, Cyprus, Greece, Macedonia, Romania, Turkey, Uzbekistan	69
16. Vietnamese	China, Vietnam	67.7
17. Telugu	India, Singapore	66.4
18. Chinese, Yue (Cantonese)	Brunei, China, Costa Rica, Indonesia, Malaysia, Panama, Philippines, Singapore, Thailand, Vietnam	66

19. Marathi	India	64.8
20. Tamil	India, Malaysia, Mauritius, Singapore, S. Africa, Sri Lanka	63.1
21. Italian	Croatia, Eritrea, France, Italy, San Marino, Slovenia, Switzerland	59
22. Urdu	Afghanistan, India, Mauritius, Pakistan, S. Africa, Thailand	58
23. Chinese, Min Nan	Brunei, China, Indonesia, Malaysia, Philippines, Singapore, Taiwan, Thailand	49
24. Chinese, Jinyu	China	45
25. Gujarati	India, Kenya, Pakistan, Singapore, S. Africa, Tanzania, Uganda, Zimbabwe	44
26. Polish	Czech Rep., Germany, Israel, Poland, Romania, Slovakia	44
27. Ukrainian	Poland, Slovakia, Ukraine	41
28. Persian	Iran, Iraq, Afghanistan, Oman, Qatar, Tajikistan, U A Emirates	37.3
29. Chinese, Xiang	China	36
30. Malayalam	India, Singapore	34
31. Chinese, Hakka	Brunei, China, Indonesia, Malaysia, Panama, Singapore, Suriname, Taiwan, Thailand	34
32. Kannada	India	33.7
33. Oriya	India	31
34. Panjabi, Western	India, Pakistan	30
35. Sunda	Indonesia	27
36. Panjabi, Eastern	India, Kenya, Singapore	26
37. Romanian	Hungary, Israel, Moldova, Romania, Serbia and Montenegro, Ukraine	26
38. Bhojpuri	India, Mauritius, Nepal	25

39.	Azerbaijani, South	Afghanistan, Iran, Iraq, Syria, Turkey	24.4
40.	Maithili	India, Nepal	24.3
41.	Hausa	Benin, Burkina Faso, Cameroon, Ghana, Niger, Nigeria, Sudan, Togo	24.2
42.	Burmese	Bangladesh, Myanmar	22
43.	Serbo–Croatian	Bosnia and Herzegovina, Croatia, Macedonia, Serbia and Montenegro, Slovenia	21
44.	Chinese, Gan	China	20.6
45.	Awadhi	India, Nepal	20.5
46.	Thai	Singapore, Thailand, Malaysia	20
47.	Dutch	Belgium, France, Netherlands, Suriname	20
48.	Yoruba	Benin, Nigeria	20
49.	Sindhi	Afghanistan, India, Pakistan, Singapore	19.7

9 Religions

Religions of the World

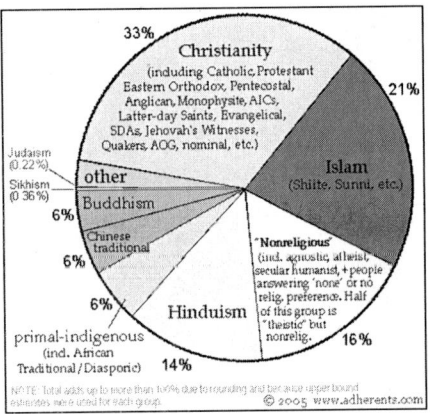

There are twelve classical world religions—those religions most often included in history of world religion surveys and studied in world religions classes: Baha'i, Buddhism, Christianity, Confucianism, Hinduism, Islam, Jainism, Judaism, Shinto, Sikhism, Taoism, and Zoroastrianism.

Hinduism Facts

1. The word 'Hinduism' is derived from the river Sindhu which was pronounced by Persians as Hindu. The region of the Indus valley is called Hindustan, and thus the religion of the Indus valley is called Hinduism.

2. Goal of life: To attain self-realisation
3. All beings have a soul; advanced souls take bodies with higher abilities like that of humans. All souls evolve up the ladder
4. God is called Satchidananda: Ever existing, Ever conscious, Ever new bliss
5. There has been no known founder of Hinduism, Hinduism derives its practices form ancient sages to today's saints, there has been a tradition of sages and saints from thousands of years, at least for last 10,000 years
6. Hinduism is the oldest religion among the existing larger religions
7. Hinduism believes in one god many forms. People chose the form through which they wanted to seek god, thus there are so many gods
8. Hindus worship many gods; Shiva, Krishna, Rama, Durga, Kali are among the most worshiped forms of god
9. Hinduism is the world's 3rd largest religion with more than 900,000,000 followers
10. Hinduism originated in India
11. There is no specific higher authority or governing body that is responsible for the religion
12. Countries where most of the Hindu population is concentrated are India, Nepal, Bangladesh, Indonesia, Sri Lanka and Pakistan
13. God is considered both male and female, or as the one who has no sex or both.
14. Scriptures are divided into shrutis (those which were heard by sages in deep meditation) and smritis (those which were recorded or memorised)
15. Vedas are the known ancient Hindu scriptures. Other famous scriptures are Upanishads, Bhagavad Gita, Agamas, Puranas.
16. Ramayana and Mahabharata are considered as the documentation of the history of India during the times of Rama and Krishna respectively.
17. Bhagavad Gita is considered by most as the holy book of Hindus. however it is not considered as the only book.

18. Dharma, Karma and Reincarnation are the most discussed among Hindu topics
19. AUM is considered as the holy sound, because it is believed that consciousness manifested itself as form through the sound AUM

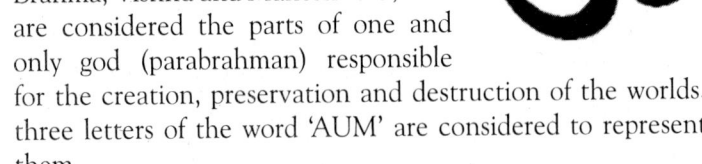

20. There are three foremost deities: Brahma, Vishnu and Maheshwara, who are considered the parts of one and only god (parabrahman) responsible for the creation, preservation and destruction of the worlds. three letters of the word 'AUM' are considered to represent them.
21. Temples are the places where Hindus worship the deities, many people have altars/rooms in their houses for worship.
22. Rama and Krishna are the most celebrated historic persons who are well known for their adherence to dharma even at difficult times.
23. Places that are considered holy by the Hindus are Varanasi, Allahabad (prayag), Haridwar, Rishikesh, Ayodya, Dwaraka, Badrinath, Kedarnath, Gangotri, Nashik, Ujjaini, Puri, Rameshwaram
24. Popular festivals are: Diwali, Maha Shivaratri, Holi, Ram Navami, Krishna Janmastami, Ganesh Chaturthi, Ugadi. Different groups give importance to different festivals
25. There are three sects in Hinduism: Shaiva, Vaishnava and Shakti. But they are not definite sects, person of one sect may follow the philosophy of the other sect. Though all sects worship all gods primary importance is mostly given to one's own sect.
26. Yoga, Pranayama, Meditation, Vastu, Jyotish, Tantra, Astrology are the main contributions of Hindu system to the modern world
27. The word AUM is the main symbol of Hinduism
28. Sanskrit is the mother language of all indian languages. Most of the scriptures of Hinduism are in Sanskrit
29. Rigveda is the one of the oldest literatures

30. Knowledge is transferred from enlightened guru to disciple
31. Varanasi is the oldest city of India and also considered as the most holy of the places. After death people are either cremated or buried
32. Wedding has been in practice from 1000s of years: Monogamy is the most practiced way. Polygamy and Polyandry are also practiced though rarely. Vedas suggest that one may marry as many as one can satisfy (materially, providing all necessities) and equal to other spouses
33. One can worship God through idols/images
34. Manu Smriti is the first book written on Codes of Good conduct. Some of the codes from this are followed even today (mostly because they are relevant even today and good codes are often relevant all the time)
35. Mahabharat the most revered book of India is 10 times larger than Iliad and Odyssey combined together
36. Kumbhamela (spiritual gathering of both householders and renunciates) which occurs every 3 years is the largest gathering of humans on the earth
37. Buddhism, Jainism, Sikkhism originated from Hinduism, all these religions share lots of common philosophies
38. Cow, elephant, snake, peacock are closely associated with the religion
39. Fully blossomed Lotus flower is used a symbol of enlightenment, also as the symbol of open heart (full of love)
40. All books that contain knowledge are considered sacred
41. Number 12 is considered special, Poorna kumbha mela is celebrated every 12 years, it is believed that spiritual progress happens in practitioners in the cycle of 12 years. i.e it takes 12 years of disciplined practice to change a habit. Mantras, Japas and pranayama's are practiced in multiples of 12
42. Touching water is accepted as spiritual; it is believed that the water has positive vibrations and also the ability to pass it on.
43. There are six philosophical schools which consider Vedas as the authoritative text, they are:
    - Samkhya
    - Yoga

- Nyaya or logic
- Vaisheshika, an empiricist school of atomism
- Mimamsa, an anti-ascetic school
- Vedanta, the school where knowledge section of the Vedas is given more importance.

44. There are also three other schools which do not necessarily include Vedas in their teachings, they are:
    - Carvaka
    - Jainism
    - Buddhism

45. Ways to attain self-realisation/ways of yoga:
    - Bhakti Yoga: The path of devotion
    - Jnana yoga: The path of wisdom, where logic and rationality are considered the means to attain realization
    - Karma yoga: The path of right action, where dharmic actions are considered the means on self realisation
    - Raja Yoga: As explained by its proponent Patanjali, attaining self realization is possible by directing mind and senses towards god through the practice of Yama, Niyama, Asana (right posture/sitting position), Pranayama (control of life energy), Pratyahara (directing senses inward), Dharana (concentration), Dhyana (meditation) and Samadhi

46. Three important aspects of the supreme god:
    - Brahma: the creator, the creating aspect
    - Vishnu: the preserver, the preserving aspect
    - Maheshwara: the destroyer, the destroying aspects

47. Three important schools of Vedanta:
    - Advaita: Shankaracharya the proponent of Advaita explains there is non-duality between the individual soul and the supreme soul.
    - Dvaita: Madhvacharya the proponent of Dvaita explains that the soul and supreme soul are separate though the soul is from the supreme soul.
    - Vishishtadvaita: Ramanujacharya the proponent of Vishishtadvaita explains soul to be the individual entity

48. Though there are slight differences in these three views, these are agreed upon as three different views of the same truth rather than three different truths (they all agree upon soul, karma, reincarnation and supreme soul concepts primary difference is in the relationship between soul and supreme soul and in their oneness)
49. Trigunas/Three modes of nature:
    - Sattva: Pure and good nature
    - Rajas: passion and activating nature
    - Tamas: Inertia, indifference and darkness
50. Every person has these three qualities to different degrees.
51. Four objectives of life (purusharthas):
    - Dharma: adherence to righteousness
    - Artha: to gain prosperity (through righteous means)
    - Kama: to quench passions (through righteous means)
    - Moksha: To attain liberation from rebirth
52. Moksha is considered the highest and final goal. Every one (who is also into acquiring wealth and objects of passion) is suggested to follow Dharma, because Dharma is believed to be the highest way to freedom from bondage.
53. Four Vernas/Four classes: people are classified into four classes according to their natural mental inclinations and abilities, in recent years it has been misunderstood and people are classified by their birth
    - Brahmana: (predominantly Sattva) Those who are naturally inclined towards attaining self-realisation and in helping others towards god. It comprises of saints, sages, yogis and all those who are strongly adherent to dharma.
    - Kshatriya: (predominantly Rajas) Those who are naturally into action and passions. It comprises of kings, soldiers (sports persons, athletes can be grouped into this).
    - Vaishyas: (predominantly both Rajas and tamas) Those whose primary inclination is towards attaining wealth. Comprises of farmers, merchants, and businessmen.
    - Shudras: (predominantly tamas) Those who undertake hard labor for living. Comprises of servants and labourers.

54. Four Ashramas/Four stages of life:
    - Brahmacharya: Early stage of life which is spent in learning arts of life and spirituality.
    - Grihastha: Householder life, where earning for livelihood, taking care of children and parents are of primary importance.
    - Vanaprastha: Retirement stage, where transfer of responsibilities and duties to younger generation is advised
    - Sanyasa: renunciation stage, in this stage one renounces all worldly attachments and moves to a quiet place to practice spirituality very seriously until death
55. Four ages/Four Yugas: According to the distance of the planet from the Center of the creation (Vishnu Nabhi) time is divided into four ages. Inhabitants of the planet will have higher abilities and life span when the planet is closer to the centre of creation.
    - Satya Yuga/Krita yuga (Golden age): People are predominantly righteous, world will be 100 per cent righteous in this age humans have very high life span
    - Treta Yuga: World will be 75 per cent righteous in this age. life span of humans is still high
    - Dwapara Yuga: World will be 50 per cent righteous, life span is considerably decreased but still high.
    - Kali Yuga: world is 25 per cent righteous. Life span of humans in 120 years
56. It is said that in higher ages advanced souls prefer to incarnate, and vice versa.
57. Reincarnation: Beings after they die enter astral world, they enter the physical body according to their past tendencies. Those souls which have burnt all tendencies do not have to take rebirth. Those who intentionally take birth to help other souls to advance spiritually are called 'avatars'. Rama, Krishna, Buddha, Jesus can be considered avatars.
58. Karma: Karma is the accumulation of fruits of actions. Among different types of karma psychological Karma can be easily understood. Psychological Karma is essentially 'The way we

train our mind to act is how it is going to act'. Karma has bigger effect on our decisions.

Some Practices:

- Elders are respected.
- Families do not divide unless necessary. Father and son live together.
- Daughters leave the house to live with their husbands.
- One cleans his face and foot before entering temples.
- One does not wear shoes or footwear inside the temple.
- Men and women wear sacred ash (Vibhuti) or kumkum on forehead, to help them concentrate between the eyes, practicing which frees the mind gradually from tendencies.
- Women wear bangles, bindi or kumkum, Mangalya (as a sign after wedding), earrings, nose-jewel and toe ring (also after wedding).
- Women decorate their hairs by adorning flowers.
- There is no definite dress code, but there is usually a followed dress type from time to time.
- Renunciates wear ochre/saffron dress to symbolize the renunciation.
- Celibacy is advocated until the marriage.

10 Food

India – The Land of Spices

- India is rightly called the Land of Spices. No country in the world produces as many varieties of spices as India.
- Greek, Roman and Arab traders have contributed a lot to the first foreign flavours in Indian cuisine.
- Staple ingredients of Indian cuisine like potato, tomato and chilli don't have Indian origin. They were brought to India by the Portuguese.
- The Portuguese also introduced the Indians to refined sugar. Fruits and honey were used as sweeteners in Indian food.
- Chicken Tikka Masala, a popular dish in India, is not Indian. It was invented in Glasgow, Scotland!
- The first Indian restaurant in the USA was opened in the mid 1960s. Today, there are around 80,000 Indian restaurants in America.
- Very little is known about the food and eating habits of the earliest Indian civilisation, Indus Valley civilisation, because the ancient language has not been deciphered yet.
- According to Indian Food Theory, our food has 6 different flavours: sweet, salty, bitter, sour, astringent and spicy.
- A proper Indian meal is a perfect balance of all 6 flavours, with one or two flavours standing out.
- Chutneys: Indian food is incomplete without this delicious side dish. But do you know the Britishers' loved Indian chutneys as

much as Indians do. In fact, they named one of the chutneys as 'Major Grey's'. It is still sold in India and is quite famous.

- Mithais are an important part of Indian cuisine and celebrations. Payasam, one of the favourite sweet dishes of South India, is a must-serve at important ceremonies like weddings. According to South Indian tradition, a wedding is not over until Payasam is served.
- Traditional Kashmiri cooking, Wazwan, reflects strong Central Asian influence. The unique thing about this cooking technique is that the spices are boiled, not fried. It gives the food a distinctive flavour and aroma.
- Pepper is known as the king of spices because it goes well with everything. Mixed with salt and it becomes the classic combination we all love.
- Dum pulao or dum biryani…This style of cooking originated in India: The Nawab of Awadh was facing a shortage of food in his region so he ordered a meal to be cooked for all the poor in huge handis,(utensils) covered with a lid and sealed with dough. This would help cook a lot of food with minimum resources, but who would have thought that this would eventually lead to a new style of cooking, now known as 'dum'.
- Indian food system classifies food into three categories—Saatvic (fresh vegetables and juice), Raajsic (oily and spicy food) and Taamsic (Meat and liquor). They believe:
  - Saatvic food leads you to higher states of consciousness.
  - Raajsic food is the foundation of activity and motion.
  - Taamsic food brings out negative feelings.

Some National Dishes

- Quaboli Palaw: National Dish of Afghanistan
- Qofte Ferguara (Fried Meatballs)—National Dish of Albania
- Gescudella De Pages (Country Stew)—National Dish of Andorra
- Doro Wat—National Dish of Angola
- Saffron & Raisin Couscous With Fresh Mint—National Dish of Algeria

- Luau/Palusami—National Dish of American Samoa
- Carbonada Criolla Stew With Meat, Vegetables, and Fruit—The National Dish is Beef, This is a Favorite Beef Stew.—National Dish of Argentina
- Khash or Pacha—Hoof, Stomach and Tongue Stew—National Dish of Armenia
- Australian Meat Pie—National Dish of Australia
- Wiener Schnitzel Mit Beilagen—National Dish of Austria
- Yapaq Dolmasi—National Dish of Azerbaijan
- Chicken Korma—National Dish of Bangladesh
- Draniki—(Potato Pancakes)—National Dish of Belarus
- Carbonnades Flamandes (Belgian Beef Stew with Beer)—National Dish of Belgium
- Ema Datshi—(Chili and Cheese Stew)—National Dish of Bhutan
- Picante De Pollo (Chicken in a Spicy Sauce)—National Dish of Bolivia
- Cevapcici—Excellent when Served as a Sandwich—National Dish of Bosnia
- Feijoada—National Dish of Brazil
- Fish and Chips—National Dish of Britain
- Monastery Gyuvetch—National Dish of Bulgaria
- Amok—National Dish of Cambodia
- Poutine—National Dish of Canada
- Pastel De Choclo and Chilean Sea Bass—National Dish of Chile
- Peking Duck—(Beijing)—National Dishes of China
- Ajiaco (Colombian Stew)—National Dish of Colombia
- Gallo Pinto Con Platanos Fritos—National Dish of Costa Rica
- Istrian Yota (Stew)—National Dish of Croatia
- Arroz Con Pollo—National Dish of Cuba
- Fasolada (Sailor's Bean Soup)—National Dish of Cyprus
- Vepro–Knedlo–Zelo–(Pork Roast–Dumplings–Cabbage–Gravy)—National Dish of the Czech Republic
- Frickadeller—National Dish of Denmark

- Chicharrones De Pollo—National Dish of the Dominican Republic
- Ecuadorian Ceviche'—National Dish of Ecuador
- Ful Medames—National Dish of Egypt
- Papusa (Pupusa)—National Dish of El Salvador
- Yet'ef Injera & Doro Wat—National Dishes of Ethiopia
- Fijian Kokoda—National Dish of Fiji
- Karelian Pasties—National Dish of Finland
- Pot Au Feu—National Dish of France
- Bratwurst, Sauerkraut, Mashed Potatoes, and Roasted Onions—National Dishes of Germany
- Moussaka—National Dish of Greece
- Fiambre—National Dish of Guatemala
- Goulash (Gulyasleves)—National Dish of Hungary
- Tandoori Chicken—National Dish of India
- Gado Gado—National Dish of Indonesia
- Chelow Kebab—(Rice and Kabab)—National Dish of Iran
- Simach Maskuf (Masgoof)—National Dish of Iraq
- Colcannon, Irish Stew—National Dish of Ireland
- Falafel—National Dish of Israel
- Pasta—National Dish of Italy
- Ackee and Saltfish—National Dish of Jamaica
- Sushi, Ramen, Soba Noodles, Udon—National Dishes of Japan
- Mansaf—National Dish of Jordan
- Beshkarmak—National Dish of Kazakhstan
- Ugali—National Dish of Kenya
- Kim Chee—National Dish of North Korea
- Bulgogi, Kim Chee, Bibimbap, Naengmyeon—National Dishes of South Korea
- Makbous Dajaj—National Dish of Kuwait
- Laab—National Dish of Laos
- Kibbeh—National Dish of Lebanon
- Fufu (Dumboy)—National Dish of Liberia
- Cuscus Bil–Bosla—National Dish of Libya

- Cepelinai—National Dish of Lithuania
- Nasi Lemak (Coconut Flavoured Rice Dish)—National Dish of Malaysia
- Burrito, Taco, Mole, Chile Rellenos, Chiles En Nogada—National Dishes of Mexico
- Pan Bagnat—National Dish of Monaco
- Moroccan Tagine and Couscous in the Fez Style With Seven Vegetables—National Dish of Morocco
- Frango A Portuguesa – National Dish of Mozambique
- Mohinga—National Dish of Myanmar
- Daal Bhaat Tarkaari (Lentils, Rice, Vegetable Curry)—National Dish of Nepal
- Stamppot—National Dish of Netherlands
- Pavlova—National Dish of New Zealand
- Lutefisk—National Dish of Norway
- Ceviche', Cebiche', or Seviche'—National Dish of Peru
- Chicken–Adobo—Filipino Chicken with Garlic—National Dish of the Phillipines
- Bigos—National Dish of Poland
- Bacalhau (Salted Codfish)—National Dish of Portugal
- Flaggandules (Rice With Pigeon Peas)—National Dish of Puerto Rico
- Siberian Pelmeny—National Dish of Russia/Siberia
- Kapsa (Chicken & Rice)—National Dish of Saudi Arabia
- Singapore Chicken Rice—National Dish of Singapore
- Doro Wat—National Dish of South Africa
- Paella, Tortilla De Patatas, Tapas—National Dishes of Spain
- Fuul—National Dish of Sudan
- Swedish Meatballs—National Dish of Sweden
- Kibbeh (Bulghur Meatballs)—National Dish of Syria
- Pad Thai—National Dish of Thailand
- Tunisian Cous Cous—National Dish of Tunisia
- Doner Kebab—National Dish of Turkey
- Cherry Varenniki (Cherry Dumplings)—National Dish of Ukraine

- Thanksgiving Turkey, Pumpkin Pie, Hamburger, Hot Dog, Doughnut, Apple Pie—National Dish of United States of America
- Plov (Rice Pilaf)—National Dish of Uzbekistan
- Pho Bo (Beef Noodle Soup)—National Dish of Vietnam

11 Sports

National Sports of Countries

A national sport is a sport or game that is considered to be an intrinsic part of the culture of a nation. Some sports are national sports as established by the law of the country, while others are popularly accepted as national sports.

Country	Sport
Afghanistan	Buzkashi
Anguilla	Yacht racing
Antigua and Barbuda	Cricket
Argentina	Pato
Australia	Cricket, AFL
Bahamas	Sloop sailing
Bangladesh	Kabaddi
Barbados	Cricket
Bermuda	Cricket
Bhutan	Archery
Brazil	Capoeira
Canada	Lacrosse (summer), Ice hockey (winter)
Chile	Chilean rodeo
China	Table Tennis
Colombia	Tejo

Czech Republic	Ice hockey
Dominican Republic	Baseball
England	Cricket
Estonia	Basketball
Finland	Pesäpallo
Georgia	Rugby union
Grenada	Cricket
Guyana	Cricket
Haiti	Football
Hungary	Football or Water polo
Iran	Varzesh–e Bastani (wrestling)
Ireland	Gaelic games
Israel	Football
Italy	Football
Jamaica	Cricket
Japan	Sumo Wrestling
Latvia	Basketball (summer), Ice hockey (winter)
Lithuania	Basketball
Madagascar	Rugby union
Mauritius	Football
Mexico	Charrería
Mongolia	Archery, Mongolian wrestling, Horse racing
Nepal	Dandi Biyo
New Zealand	Rugby Union
Norway	Cross–country skiing
Pakistan	Field Hockey
Papua New Guinea	Rugby league
Peru	Paleta Frontón
Philippines	Arnis

Poland	Football
Puerto Rico	Baseball, Paso Fino
Romania	Oina
Russia	Bandy
Scotland	Golf
Serbia	Banatske Šore
Slovenia	Alpine skiing
South Korea	Taekwondo
Spain	Football
Sri Lanka	Volleyball
Turkey	Oil wrestling & Cirit
Turks and Caicos Islands	Cricket
United States	Baseball
Uruguay	Destrezas Criollas (Creole Skills)
Venezuela	Baseball
Wales	Rugby union

INSIDE OUT

USA – Baseball
Canada – Ice Hockey
India – Hockey
Bangladesh – Kabaddi
Russia – Football and Chess
Brazil – Football
England – Cricket
Australia – Cricket
Malaysia – Badminton
Indonesia – Badminton
Switzerland – Shooting and Gymnastics

Spain – Bulls Fighting
New Zealand – Rugby Union
Pakistan – Field Hockey
Srilanka – Volley ball
China – Table Tennis
France – Football
Japan – Judo
Pakistan – Hockey
Scotland – Rugby Football
Bhutan – Archery
Turkey – Wrestling and Jereed

The Olympics

The early Olympic Games were celebrated as a religious festival from 776 B.C. until 393 A.D., when the games were banned for being a pagan festival (the Olympics celebrated the Greek god Zeus). In 1894, a French educator Baron Pierre de Coubertin, proposed a revival of the ancient tradition, and thus the modern-day Olympic Summer Games were born.

- Host Greece won the most medals (47) at the first Olympic Summer Games in 1896.
- The first Winter Olympic Games were held in Chamonix, France in 1924.
- Norway has won the most medals (263) at the Winter Games.
- The United States has won more medals (2,189) at the Summer Games than any other country.
- The five Olympic rings represent the five major regions of the world—Africa, the Americas, Asia, Europe and Oceana—and every national flag in the world includes one of the five colours, which are (from left to right) blue, yellow, black, green, and red.
- Up until 1994 the Olympics were held every four years. Since then, the Winter and Summer games have alternated every two years.
- The first Olympics covered by U.S. television was the 1960 Summer Games in Rome by CBS.
- No country in the Southern Hemisphere has ever hosted a Winter Games.
- Three continents—Africa, South America, and Antarctica—have never hosted an Olympics.
- A record 202 countries participated in the 2004 Olympic Summer Games in Athens.
- Only four athletes have ever won medals at both the Winter and Summer Olympic Games: Eddie Eagan (United States),

Jacob Tullin Thams (Norway), Christa Luding–Rothenburger (East Germany), and Clara Hughes (Canada).

- Speed skater Bonnie Blair has won six medals at the Olympic Winter Games. That's more than any other American athlete.
- Nobody has won more medals at the Winter Games than cross-country skier Bjorn Dählie of Norway, who has 12.
- Larrisa Latynina, a gymnast from the former Soviet Union, finished her Summer Olympic Games career with 18 total medals—the most in history.
- The United States Olympic Committee established the U.S. Olympic Hall of Fame in 1983 to recognise outstanding American Olympic athletes, however, a plan to build a hall has been suspended due to lack of funding.
- The Summer Olympic sports are archery, badminton, basketball, beach volleyball, boxing, canoe / kayak, cycling, diving, equestrian, fencing, field hockey, gymnastics, handball, judo, modern pentathlon (shooting, fencing, swimming, show jumping, and running), mountain biking, rowing, sailing, shooting, soccer, swimming, synchronised swimming, table tennis, taekwondo, tennis, track and field, triathlon (swimming, biking, running), volleyball, water polo, weightlifting, and wrestling.
- The Winter Olympic sports are alpine skiing, biathlon (cross-country skiing and target shooting), bobsled, cross-country skiing, curling, figure skating, freestyle skiing, ice hocky, luge, Nordic combined (ski jumping and cross-country skiing), skeleton, ski jumping, snowboarding, and speed skating.

More Facts

- The Beijing Olympics, 2008, began at exactly 8:08:08 PM on 8/8/08 because the number 8 is considered lucky in China.
- The Berlin 1936 Olympiad was the first games to be televised.
- There is a study of the 2004 Athens Olympics which shows that athletes who wore red while competing in 'combat sports', such as wrestling, scored higher than opponents wearing blue.

Very interesting but no scientific evidence can be produced.
- It wasn't until 1900 that women were allowed to participate in the Olympic Games.
- In 1928 Australian rower, Henry Pearce, stopped halfway through his quarter-final race to let a family of ducks pass in front of his boat. The French competition overtook him, but Pearce managed to get back in front and win the gold.
- Pierre de Coubertin, the late founder of the International Olympic Committee [IOC], decided to send his heart to the site of ancient Olympia in Greece, where it is kept in a monument. The rest of him is buried in Lausanne, Switzerland.
- No boxing was held at the 1912 Stockholm Olympics because the sport was illegal in Sweden.
- George Patton, who would later become a famous U.S. general, competed in the 1912 Stockholm Olympics pentathlon, an event combining pistol shooting, swimming, fencing, cross country and steeplechase. Patton performed poorly in his best event, pistols, but shined in fencing, defeating the French army champion. 'Old Blood and Guts' finished fifth overall, the only non–Swede to make the top seven.
- During the 1972 Munich Summer Olympics, Olga Korbut, the gymnast from the USSR was the cynosure of all. She was 17 years old and only stood 4ft 11in tall. [1.49 metres].
- Tug-o-war made its last appearance as an Olympic sport in 1920.
- French athletes bent the rules at the 1932 Los Angeles Olympics: despite 'Prohibition', they were allowed wine with their meals.
- The greatest star of the 1936 Berlin Olympics Jesse Owens, was the 10th child born to an Alabama sharecropper family named Owens. He was not born with the name Jesse, he was called James Cleveland Owens, and as a child moved to his namesake city: Cleveland. A teacher asked his name, and he said 'J.C'. The teacher thought he said 'Jesse', and the boy was too polite to disagree.
- Another great Olympian, with Chicago ties, was Johnny

Weissmuller, the winner of five gold medals in swimming who later starred as Tarzan in the movies. Weissmuller was training on the lakefront with his brother Peter when a sudden storm swamped the pleasure boat Favorite. The disaster killed 27 of the 71 people aboard, mostly women and children, but the Weissmuller brothers rescued 11 people. He can really be considered a hero.

- Ethiopian marathoner, Abebe Bikila, was the first man to successfully defend the marathon title [1960 and 1964]. An interesting observation was that he only wore shoes for the second victory.
- Romanian gymnast Nadia Comaneci scored perfect 10's seven times at the 1976 Montreal games.
- Discus thrower, Al Oerter, of the USA is the only athlete to win his event in four consecutive Olympic Games. He won gold medals and set new discus records in the 1956, 1960, 1964 and 1968 games. Only nine other athletes have even won their events twice in succession in track and field competition.
- Poland's Stella Walsh, [Stanislawa Walasiewicz] won the women's 100m race at the 1932 Olympics in Los Angeles, becoming the first woman to break the 12 second barrier. When she was killed in 1980, as an innocent victim in a robbery attempt, an autopsy declared her to be a male.

Olympic Marathon

- The reason the extra yards were added to the running distance of the marathon to make the total length a rather strange figure of 26 miles and 385 yards was because of the rather whimsical demand of Queen Alexandra of Great Britain, who demanded, in 1908, that the marathon should end below the royal box at London's White City Stadium, which added the extra 385 yards.

- The First Marathon: In 490 BCE, Pheidippides, a Greek soldier, ran from Marathon to Athens [about 25 miles] to inform the Athenians the outcome of the battle with invading Persians. The distance was filled with hills and other obstacles; thus Pheidippides arrived in Athens exhausted and with bleeding feet. After telling the townspeople of the Greeks' success in the battle, Pheidippides fell to the ground dead. In 1896, at the first modern Olympic Games, held a race of approximately the same length in commemoration of Pheidippides.

Quotable quote

The most important thing in the Olympic Games is not winning but taking part; the essential thing in life is not conquering but fighting well. – Pierre de Coubertin (primarily responsible for the revival of the Olympic Games in 1894)

The London Olympiad 2012

- Hiroshi Hoketsu, 71, is the oldest ever competitor at a Games. He appeared in the men's equestrian event at London 2012, 48 years since his first Olympic appearance at the 1964 Tokyo Games.
- Over 800,000 people used public transport to travel to the Games.
- 17km of steel wires are used for the Velodrome's cable roof; that's twice the height of Mount Everest
- 90 per cent of the material inside the Olympic park can be reused or recycled, making this the greenest Olympics yet.
- 26,400 tennis balls were used.
- 65,000 towels were used by the athletes.
- 2,700 footballs were used.
- London hosts the Olympic Games in 2012: they became the

first city to be officially listed as hosting the Games three times: 1908, 1948 and 2012. (Athens was host in 1896, 1906 and 2004, but the Intercalated games of 1906 were de–listed as being 'Olympic Games'.)

2016 Olympics

The first Paralympic Games was held at London in 1948. The name 'Paralympics' comes from the words 'Parallel' and 'Olympics'.

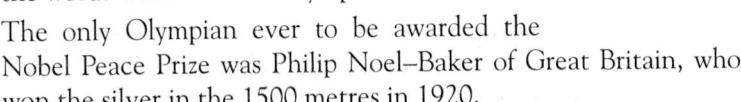

The only Olympian ever to be awarded the Nobel Peace Prize was Philip Noel–Baker of Great Britain, who won the silver in the 1500 metres in 1920.

The Olympic Torch

The Olympic torch passes through all 5 continents on its 79 day journey.
a. 1896 – First Olympics of the Modern Era.
b. 1936 – Berlin – Hitler Olympics.
c. 1984 – Los Angeles – Commercialisation takes off.

Olympic Medals

- At the first modern Olympic Games in Athens in 1896, silver medals were awarded to the winners and bronze to the second place getters.
- Olympic gold medals haven't been pure gold in years. The 1912 Olympics was the last time that gold medals were solid gold. Ever since, they've been silver with gold plating.
- Starting in Amsterdam 1928, all Summer Olympic medals featured the same design: a Greek goddess, the Olympic Rings, the Coliseum of ancient Athens, a Greek vase, a horse-drawn chariot. Each host city then adds their own design together with the year and the number of Olympiad. The host city has control over the design of the reverse side of the medal.
- In 1900, in France, Olympian winners got paintings instead of gold medals. Gold, silver and bronze medals weren't given out

until the third modern Olympics in 1904. The French gave the winners paintings because they believed they were more valuable.

- Incidentally, more athletes than spectators attended the 1900 Paris Olympic Games.

Top 10 Olympic Athletes from Track and Field Olympic

1. Jim Thorpe – 1912 Stockholm Decathlon and Pentathlon gold.
2. Paavo Nurmi (Flying Finn) – 1920 Antwerp: 10,000m. Also 1924 Paris: 10,000m, 5,000m.
3. Mildred (Babe) Didrikson – 1932 Los Angeles gold medal in the javelin and 80m hurdles.
4. Jesse Owens – 1936 Berlin 100, 400m, long jump 100m relay.
5. Emil Zátopek – 1952 Helsinki 5,000m, 10,000m, marathon.
6. Al Oerter – Discus gold medal: 1956, 1960, 1964 and 1968.
7. Bob Beamon – 1968 Mexico City long jump.
8. Carl Lewis – 1984 Los Angeles 100, 400m, long jump 100m relay. Also long jump 1988, 1992 and 1996.
9. Michael Johnson – 1992 Barcelona 200m and 400m. Also 1996 400m.
10. Usain Bolt – 2008 Beijing.

Top 10 Olympic Champions from Swimming and Water Sports

1. Duke Paoa Kahanamoku – 1912: 100m freestyle.
2. Anita Lonsbrough – 1960 Rome: 200m breaststroke.
3. Dawn Fraser – 1956, 1960, 1964: 100m freestyle.
4. Mark Spitz – 1972 Munich seven gold medals.
5. Greg Louganis – 1988 Seoul. Qualified for the springboard final despite hitting his head on the board. He went on to win the final, to follow up his achievement of winning the same event 4 years earlier.
6. Kristin Otto – 1988 Seoul
7. Jennifer Beth Thompson – 1992, 1996, 2000 and 2004
8. Ian Thorpe – 2000 Sydney: 400m freestyle.
9. Steve Redgrave rowing. Won gold medals at 5 consecutive Olympiads 1984, 1988, 1992, 1996, 2000.

10. Michael Phelps – 2008 Beijing. Won 8 gold medals, most ever at one Olympiad. He also won 6 golds in Athens in 2004.

> **Top Olympic Gymnasts**
> - Olga Korbut – 1972 Munich
> - Nadia Comaneci – 1996 Montreal. Scored seven perfect 10s on her way to three gold medals

12 World Literature

Epics of the World

The Great Epics of the World
- Mahabharata by Vyasa (Sanskrit)
- The Iliad by Homer (Greek)
- The Odyssey by Homer (Greek)
- Orlando furioso by Ludovico Ariosto (Italian epic)
- Ramayana by Valmiki (Sanskrit)
- The Divine Comedy by Dante Alighieri (Italian epic)
- Beowulf Anonymous (Old English)
- Paradise Lost by John Milton (English)

The Great Epics of the World

Mahabharata by Vyasa (Sanskrit)

Mahabharata is one of the great Indian epic compiled around 8th century BC. This epic poem has about one lakh couplets in Sanskrit and it can be considered as the longest epic poem of the world. This ancient epic deals with the rivalry between cousins—

Kauravas and Pandavas—of a great ruling family of India. The armies of the two groups meet at the battleground at Kurushetra in which the Pandavas can destroy the Kauravas. The epic consists of thousands of mythical and historical stories.

The Iliad by Homer (Greek)

Iliad is one of the most celebrated and well known epics of the world. It is believed to be written by in 9th century BC by Homer. This poem is based on the legend of Trojan War. Iliad means the tale of ilios or the tale of troy. It narrates the story of the Greek struggle to rescue Helen, from Trojans, the wrath of Achilles and subsequent destruction of Troy.

The Odyssey by Homer (Greek)

Odyssey is believed to be written in 9th century BC by Homer the great Greek poet. It describes the exploits of the Odysseus during his homecoming after the fall of Troy. This great epic follows the Aristotelian conventions of epic poem. The poem describes the obstacles faced by Odysseus, varied tests of gods that he had undergone, his affair with nymph Calypso on the homecoming voyage, and his return to his kingdom.

Orlando Furioso by Ludovico Ariosto (Italian epic)

Orlando Furioso is a famous epic with full of supernatural, allegorical and romantic adventures. The main theme of the epic is the war between Christians and pagans. Even though Ariosto, the writer, has depended much on the Graeco–Roman literary tradition of earlier writers for characters and incidents, it is a great epic poem due to his smooth versification and technical facility which make the poem vigorous and brilliant, with ironic and humorous contrasts.

Ramayana by Valmiki (Sanskrit)

Ramayana is a great Indian epic poem written in 5th century BC. It is the oldest and most popular epic of Indian sub continent, believed to be written by Valmiki. It is written in Sanskrit, one of the earliest Indo–European languages, and has around 2400 couplets in seven sections. Ramayana means 'the journey of Rama'. It depicts the conflict between Rama, the incarnation of God Vishnu, and Ravana who can be taken as the representative of evil forces and the final victory of the God incarnated Rama in safeguarding the Dharma (Universal moral order).

The Divine Comedy by Dante Alighieri (Italian epic)

Divine Comedy is a celebrated epic poem written by Dante in 14th century. The narrator is lost in a forest. The poet narrator meets Virgil who guides him through the world after death. Virgil takes him through Hell. They go through the base of the purgatory and he can see the terraces of it where the sins of those who are ultimately to be saved are cleansed away. Then Beatrice guides him to the ultimate heaven. The poem ends with his moment of illumination and the vision of trinity.

Beowulf Anonymous (Old English)

Beowulf, one of the earliest epic of the world, is based on a Scandinavian legend. It was written around 750 AD by an anonymous writer and it has about 3000 lines.

Beowulf, the great warrior hero, saves Horthgar, the king of Danes, from the attack of Grendel, a terrible monster, by killing it. Grendel's mother attacks him to avenge the death of his son. In the fight, Beowulf kills the mother – monster also, but he gets a mortal wound in the fight and succumbs to it.

This epic, the most celebrated survival from Old English literature, is also the earliest extant poem in a modern European language.

Paradise Lost by John Milton (English)

Paradise Lost is one of the greatest English literary epic based on the theme of fall of man given in the old Testament and it was written in 17th century by John Milton. The great poet wrote it 'to justify the ways of god to man'. The epic poem begins with the Satan's devilish plans to take revenge against god for his expulsion from heaven. Some critics has opined that Milton's Satan

is the hero of the epic poem due to the excellent depiction and exposition of that character. This epic is celebrated for Milton's grand style, his interpretation of Biblical myth and Christian doctrine.

Shah Name by Firdousi (Persian)

Shah Name is great Persian epic based on the historical and mythical accounts of around fifty Persian kings. Shah Name means 'book of kings'. The epic begins the mythical creation of Persia and ends in the narration of the stories

of historical kings. The most famous story of Shah Name is about the legendary king of Rostam and Sohrab, his son.

Aeneid by Virgil (Latin)

Aeneid is a great epic which is based on the legend of Aeneas. It is Roman nationalistic and patriotic poem which narrates the evolution of great Roman empire. This poem shows great dramatic skill of high order and power of description. Aeneas decides to establish a secure kingdom for his people in Italy. During the long and perilous voyage for it their ships are wreaked on the coast of Africa. The Dido of Carthage invites them which prolongs their voyage. In the next voyage, they reach Latinum, ruled by Latinus. Aeneas marries his daughter Lavinia after killing Turanus, another suitor of her. He establishes a city of lavinium which becomes a base for great Roman empire later.

BEST–SELLING FICTION AUTHOR

Author	Min. estimated sales	Max. estimated sales	Original language	Genre or title	Number of books	Citizenship
William Shakespeare	2 billion	4 billion	English	Plays and poetry		English
Agatha Christie	2 billion	4 billion	English	Whodunits including the *Miss Marple* and *Hercule Poirot* series	85	British
Barbara Cartland	500 million	1 billion	English	Romance	723	British
Danielle Steel	500 million	800 million	English	Romance	120	American
Harold Robbins	750 million	750 million	English	Adventure	23	American
Georges Simenon	500 million	700 million	French	Detectives, *Maigret*	570	Belgian
Sidney Sheldon	370 million	600 million	English	Suspense	21	American

Author	Min. estimated sales	Max. estimated sales	Original language	Genre or title	Number of books	Citizenship
Enid Blyton	300 million	600 million	English	Children's literature, *Noddy*, *The Famous Five*, *The Secret Seven*	800	British
Dr. Seuss	100 million	500 million	English	Children's literature	44	American
Gilbert Patten	125 million	500 million	English	Adolescent adventures	209	American
J. K. Rowling	350 million	450 million	English	*Harry Potter*	11	British
Leo Tolstoy		413 million	Russian	*War and Peace*, *Anna Karenina*	48	Russian
Corín Tellado	400 million	400 million	Spanish	Romance	4,000	Spanish
Jackie Collins	250 million	400 million	English	Romance	25	British
Horatio Alger, Jr.	200 million	400 million	English	Dime novels	135	American
R. L. Stine	100 million	400 million	English	*Goosebumps* series, *Fear Street* series, horror, comedy	430+	American
Dean Koontz	325 million	400 million	English	Horror, thriller, science fiction, fantasy	91	American
Nora Roberts	145 million	400 million	English	Romance	200+	American
Alexander Pushkin		357 million	Russian	Plays, poetry, prose, *Eugene Onegin*	17	Russian
Stephen King	300 million	350 million	English	Horror, science fiction, fantasy, *It*, *The Shining*, *The Stand*, *Bag of Bones*, *Needful Things*	70	American
Louis L'Amour	230 million	330 million	English	Western	101	American
Erle Stanley Gardner	100 million	325 million	English	Mystery, *Perry Mason*	140	American
Jin Yong	100 million	300 million	Chinese	Wuxia	15	Hong Kong Chinese
Jiro Akagawa		300 million	Japanese	Mystery	500+	Japanese

Author	Min. estimated sales	Max. estimated sales	Original language	Genre or title	Number of books	Citizenship
Janet Dailey	300 million	300 million	English	Romance	93	American
Edgar Wallace		300 million	English	Detective	175	British
Robert Ludlum	110 million	290 million	English	Espionage, *Jason Bourne*	40	American
James Patterson	150 million	275 million	English	Thriller, *Alex Cross*	98	American
Frédéric Dard	200 million	270 million	French	Detective, *San Antonio*	300	Swiss
Jeffrey Archer	120 million	270 million	English	Crime thriller	30	British
Stan and Jan Berenstain	200 million	260 million	English	*Berenstain Bears*	300+	American
John Grisham	100 million	250 million	English	Legal thriller	22	American
Zane Grey		250 million	English	Western		American
Irving Wallace		250 million	English	Suspense		American
J. R. R. Tolkien	200 million	250 million	English	*The Lord of the Rings*, *The Hobbit*, classical fantasy	36	British
Karl May	100 million	200 million	German	Western, adventure	80	German
Mickey Spillane	100 million	200 million	English	Detective, *Mike Hammer*		American
C. S. Lewis	100 million	200 million	English	*The Chronicles of Narnia*, fantasy, popular theology	38	British
Kyotaro Nishimura		200 million	Japanese	Mystery	400+	Japanese
Dan Brown	200 million	200 million	English	Thriller, *Robert Langdon*	6	American
Ann M. Martin	172 million	180 million	English	*The Baby-sitters Club*	335	American
Ryotarq Shiba		180 million	Japanese	Historical	350	Japanese
Arthur Hailey	150 million	170 million	English	Thriller	11	British/Canadian
Gérard de Villiers		150 million	French	Detectives, *SAS*	170	French
Beatrix Potter	100 million	150 million	English	*Peter Rabbit*	23	British
Michael Crichton	150 million	150 million	English	Techno thriller	25	American

Author	Min. estimated sales	Max. estimated sales	Original language	Genre or title	Number of books	Citizenship
Richard Scarry	100 million	150 million	English	Illustrated children's books	250	American
Clive Cussler	40 million	150 million	English	Adventure, *Dirk Pitt*	37	American
Alistair MacLean		150 million	English	Adventure, thriller, war stories	32	British
Ken Follett	90 million	150 million	English	Spy thriller, historical thriller	30	British
Astrid Lindgren	100 million	145 million	Swedish	Children's literature	100	Swedish
Debbie Macomber	60 million	140 million	English	Romance		American
Paulo Coelho	92 million	140 million	Portuguese	*The Alchemist*		Brazilian
EL James	100 million	125 million	English	*Fifty Shades of Grey*	3	British
Eiji Yoshikawa		120 million	Japanese	*Musashi*	7	Japanese
Catherine Cookson	100 million	120 million	English	Romance	103	British
Stephenie Meyer	100 million	116 million	English	*The Twilight Saga, The Host*, romance	6	American
Norman Bridwell	100 million	110 million	English	*Clifford the Big Red Dog*	80	American
David Baldacci		110 million	English	Thriller	25	American
Roald Dahl	200 million	200 million	English	Children's literature	50	British
Evan Hunter	100 million	100 million	English	Detective (Ed McBain)	94	American
Andrew Neiderman	100 million	100 million	English	V. C. Andrews, *The Devil's Advocate*	60	American
Roger Hargreaves	100 million	100 million	English	Children's literature, *Mr. Men*		British
Anne Rice	75 million	100 million	English	Gothic fiction, vampires, *Interview with the Vampire* (*The Vampire Chronicles*)	27	American
Robin Cook	100 million	100 million	English	Medical thriller	27	American
Wilbur Smith	80 million	100 million	English	African adventure	32	Zambian

Author	Min. estimated sales	Max. estimated sales	Original language	Genre or title	Number of books	Citizenship
Erskine Caldwell	80 million	100 million	English	Literature	25	American
Judith Krantz	80 million	100 million	English	Romance	12	American
Eleanor Hibbert	100 million	100 million	English	Romance, historical, suspense	200	British
Lewis Carroll		100 million	English	Alice's Adventures in Wonderland, absurdist literature	5	British
Denise Robins		100 million	English	Romance	200	British
Cao Xueqin		100 million	Chinese	Dream of the Red Chamber		Chinese
Ian Fleming	100 million	100 million	English	James Bond	14	British
Hermann Hesse	100 million	100 million	German	Steppenwolf, Siddhartha, The Glass Bead Game	45	German–Swiss
Rex Stout	100 million	100 million	English	Nero Wolfe	50	American
Anne Golon	100 million	100 million	French	Angélique	14	French
Frank G. Slaughter		100 million	English	Medical	62	American
Edgar Rice Burroughs	100 million	100 million	English	Tarzan, Barsoom and Pellucidar series, science fantasy		American
John Creasey		100 million	English	Crime thriller	600	British
James Michener		100 million	English	Historical	47	American
Yasuo Uchida		100 million	Japanese	Mystery	130+	Japanese
Seiichi Morimura		100 million	Japanese	Mystery	350+	Japanese
Mary Higgins Clark	100 million	100 million	English	Thriller		American
Penny Jordan	90 million	100 million	English	Romance	200+	British
Patricia Cornwell		100 million	English	Thriller		American
Tom Clancy		100 million	English	Thriller		American

Amazing World Facts

Greatest Books of All Time

- Anna Karenina by Leo Tolstoy
- Madame Bovary by Gustave Flaubert
- War and Peace by Leo Tolstoy
- Lolita by Vladimir Nabokov
- The Adventures of Huckleberry Finn by Mark Twain
- Hamlet by William Shakespeare
- The Great Gatsby F. Scott Fitzgerald
- In Search of Lost Time by Marcel Proust
- The Stories of Anton Chekhov by Anton Chekhov
- Middlemarch by George Eliot

William Shakespeare

William Shakespeare was an English poet, playwright, and actor, widely regarded as the greatest writer in the English language and the world's pre-eminent dramatist. He is often called England's national poet, and the 'Bard of Avon'.

Greatest Russian Writers

One of greatest gifts that Russia has given to the world is its Literature. Names like Leo Tolstoy, Anton Chekov and Fyodor Dostoevsky are among the most famous Russian writers that have become household names across the globe. Their writings have been translated in several languages, and, today their novels and short stories occupy a special place in the world of classics. Here is a list of the top 10 greatest Russian writers of all times.

1. Lev Nikolayevich Tolstoy:

Lev Nikolayevich Tolstoy or most often known as Leo Tolstoy in the Anglophone world, remains one of the best writers of all time. He began his carrier as a novelist and short story writer, but later in life he also wrote some plays and essays. His most celebrated works include 'War and Peace' and 'Anna Karenina'. During different phases of his life, Tolstoy lived paradoxically. In his last days, he left home and became an ascetic, but soon died of pneumonia.

2. Fyodor Dostoevsky:

Dostoevsky, one of the greatest writers from Russia, wrote novels and short stories that explore aspects of human psychology. Graduated as a military engineer, he resigned in 1844 and joined a group of utopian socialists. He was later captured by the police and sent to Siberia. This is where the real writer was born. He described his time spent in the prison in three different novels,' The House of Dead', 'The Insulted and the Injured,' and 'Winter Notes on Summer Impression'. Apart from this, his most famous work includes 'The Idiot' and 'Crime and Punishment'.

3. Nicolai Gogol:

The Ukrainian born dramatist, short story writer and novelist, Nicolai Gogol is best known for the portrayal of real life characters in all his writings. He started his writing career with short stories, and later got immensely fascinated with the history of Ukrainian. Ultimately he obtained all the requisite information from the department of history, Kiev University. Counted among one of the greatest Russian writers of all time, he also translated his learning later into a novel, Taras Bulba.

4. Ivan Bunin:

The first Russian writer to be awarded with the Nobel Prize for Literature, Ivan Bunin was rightly considered by many as the heir to the legacy of realism by Tolstoy and Anton Chekov. His mostly widely acclaimed work includes short novels 'The Village' and the 'Dry Valley'. His autobiographical account given in the novel 'The Life of Arseniev' was another of his works that became legendary and still inspire people all around the globe.

5. Alexander Pushkin:

Alexander Pushkin rocked the Russian literary scenes with this romantic poets and novels. His first poem came at the tender age of 15, and soon he became a famous name in the Russian literature corridors. Being an emotional and sensitive person, he often gave into fights and duels. His fought almost 27 duels during his life. It was during one such duel against Georges Charles, who was trying to seduce his wife, that he lost his life.

6. Anton Chekhov:

Anton Chekov, a physician by profession, was more inclined toward writing. He initially began to write only for financial gains but soon he became more ambitious about writing seriously, while also pursuing his medical practice. To the surprise of many, this shy lad, eventually conquered the world of short stories and even today his works are taught all over the globe.

7. Mikhail Bulgakov:

One of the most controversial writers of his time, Mikhail Bulgakov, practiced medicine as early career but when he moved to Moscow, he discovered the writer in him and soon became famous for his satires on the social conditions of people in the Soviet Union. He displeased the administration with his work and that's why all of his plays were banned, and his unpublished work confiscated.

8. Vladimir Nabokov:

Vladimir Nabokov, most famously known for his novel 'Lolita', wrote in both Russian and English. His first 9 novels were in Russian, thereafter, he became more popular around the world, and so started writing novels in English. He wrote Lolita in English, and only after its huge success in Paris, he translated the book in Russian. One of the most seemingly controversial, and out of line novels, Lolita eventually attained the status of a classic and presented Nabokov as one of the greatest Russian writers of all time.

9. Ivan Turgenev:

A contemporary with Leo Tolstoy and Alexander Pushkin, Ivan Turgenev remains widely acclaimed for his novel 'Father and Sons'. He was also a short story writer and play writer. One of his most cherished short story collections is 'Sportsman's Collection'.

Initially his work, Father and Son was denounced by people in Russia, which also led to his leaving the country, but today, it is considered as one of the best classics of all time.

10. Aleksandr Solzhenitsyn:

Historian, novelist, and dramatist, Aleksandr, was a Russian writer who created awareness about the Gulag, the Soviet Union government agency that administered the labor camps, and the suppression of people living in such camps throughout the Soviet Union. Two of his most famous works include 'The Gulag Archipelago' and 'One Day in the Life of Ivan Denisovich'.

10 Greatest American Writers

1. **The Great Gatsby by F. Scott Fitzgerald (1925).** Perhaps the most searching fable of the American Dream ever written, this glittering novel of the Jazz Age paints an unforgettable portrait of its day—the flappers, the bootleg gin, the careless, giddy wealth. Self-made millionaire Jay Gatsby, determined to win back the heart of the girl he loved and lost, emerges as an emblem for romantic yearning, and the novel's narrator, Nick Carroway, brilliantly illuminates the post-World War I end to American innocence.

2. **Adventures of Huckleberry Finn by Mark Twain (1884).** Hemingway once proclaimed: All modern American literature comes from 'Huckleberry Finn'. But one can read it simply as a straightforward adventure story in which two comrades of convenience, the parentally abused rascal Huck and fugitive slave Jim, escape the laws and conventions of society on a raft trip down the Mississippi. Alternatively, it's a subversive satire in which Twain uses the only superficially naïve Huck to comment bitingly on the evils of racial bigotry, religious hypocrisy, and capitalist greed he observes in a host of other largely unsympathetic characters. Huck's climactic decision to 'light out for the Territory ahead of the rest' rather than submit to the starched standards of 'civilization' reflects a

uniquely American strain of individualism and nonconformity stretching from Daniel Boone to Easy Rider.

3. **Moby Dick by Herman Melville (1851).** This sweeping saga of obsession, vanity, and vengeance at sea can be read as a harrowing parable, a gripping adventure story, or a semi-scientific chronicle of the whaling industry. No matter, the book rewards patient readers with some of fiction's most memorable characters, from mad Captain Ahab to the titular white whale that crippled him, from the honorable pagan Queequeg to our insightful narrator/surrogate ('Call me') Ishmael, to that hell–bent vessel itself, the Pequod.

4. **The stories of Flannery O'Connor (1925–64).** Full of violence, mordant comedy, and a fierce Catholic vision that is bent on human salvation at any cost, Flannery O'Connor's stories are like no others. Bigots, intellectual snobs, shyster preachers, and crazed religious seers—a full cavalcade of what critics came to call 'grotesques'—careen through her tales, and O'Connor gleefully displays the moral inadequacy of all of them. Twentieth–century short stories often focus on tiny moments, but O'Connor's stories, with their unswerving eye for vanity and their profound sense of the sacred, feel immense.

5. **The Sound and the Fury by William Faulkner (1929).** A modernist classic of Old South decay, this novel circles the travails of the Compson family from four different narrative perspectives. All are haunted by the figure of Caddy, the only daughter, whom Faulkner described as 'a beautiful and tragic little girl.' Surrounding the trials of the family itself are the usual Faulkner suspects: alcoholism, suicide, racism, religion, money, and violence both seen and unseen. In the experimental style of the book, Quentin Compson summarizes the confused honor and tragedy that Faulkner relentlessly evokes: 'there's a curse on us its not our fault is it our fault.'

6. **Absalom, Absalom! by William Faulkner (1936).** Weaving mythic tales of biblical urgency with the experimental techniques of high modernism, Faulkner bridged the past and future. This is the story of Thomas Sutpen, a rough–hewn

striver who came to Mississippi in 1833 with a gang of wild slaves from Haiti to build a dynasty. Almost in reach, his dream is undone by plagues of biblical (and Faulknerian) proportions: racism, incest, war, fratricide, pride, and jealousy. Through the use of multiple narrators, Faulkner turns this gripping Yoknapatawpha saga into a profound and dazzling meditation on truth, memory, history, and literature itself.

7. **To Kill a Mockingbird by Harper Lee (1960).** Tomboy Scout and her brother Jem are the children of the profoundly decent widower Atticus Finch, a small-town Alabama lawyer defending a black man accused of raping a white woman. Although Tom Robinson's trial is the centerpiece of this Pulitzer Prize-winning novel—raising profound questions of race and conscience—this is, at heart, a tale about the fears and mysteries of growing up, as the children learn about bravery, empathy, and societal expectations through a series of evocative set pieces that conjure the Depression-era South.

8. **Invisible Man by Ralph Ellison (1952).** This modernist novel follows the bizarre, often surreal adventures of an unnamed narrator, a black man, whose identity becomes a battleground in racially divided America. Expected to be submissive and obedient in the South, he must decipher the often contradictory rules whites set for a black man's behaviour. Traveling north to Harlem, he meets white leaders intent on controlling and manipulating him. Desperate to seize control of his life, he imitates Dostoevsky's underground man, escaping down a manhole where he vows to remain until he can define himself. The book's famous last line, 'Who knows, but that on the lower frequencies I speak for you,' suggests how it transcends race to tell a universal story of the quest for self-determination.

9. **The Grapes of Wrath by John Steinbeck (1939).** A powerful portrait of Depression-era America, this gritty social novel follows the Joad family as they flee their farm in the Oklahoma dust bowl for the promised land of California. While limping across a crippled land, Ma and Pa Joad, their

pregnant daughter Rose of Sharon, and their recently paroled son Tom sleep in ramshackle Hoovervilles filled with other refugees and encounter hardship, death, and deceit. While vividly capturing the plight of a nation, Steinbeck renders people who have lost everything but their dignity.

10. **The Portrait of a Lady by Henry James (1881).** James's Portrait is of that superior creature Isabel Archer, an assured American girl who is determined to forge her destiny in the drawing rooms of Europe. To this end, she weds the older and more cultivated Gilbert Osmond, and eventually finds that she is less the author of her fate than she thought. Throughout, James gives us a combination of careful psychological refraction and truly diabolical plotting. The result is a book at once chilling and glorious.